THE GAP

Jack Burton is a Methodist minister and bus driver in Norwich, where he occasionally holds special services in a redundant medieval church. His book, *Transport of Delight*, won the Winifred Mary Stanford prize in 1978.

Dedicated, with Betty's permission,
to the memory of
The Revd Bernard P. Marks, B.A., B.D.

Jack Burton

The Gap

CHRISTIANS AND PEOPLE WHO DON'T GO TO CHURCH

TRI△NGLE

First published 1991
SPCK
Holy Trinity Church
Marylebone Road
London NW1 4DU

British Library Cataloguing in Publication Data

Burton, Jack, *1939–*
The gap: Christians and people who don't go to church
1. Christians. Interpersonal relationships
I. Title
261.2
ISBN 0–281–04512–7

Typeset by Inforum Typesetting, Portsmouth
Printed in Great Britain by
Courier International, Tiptree, Essex

Contents

For I could wish that myself were accursed from Christ for my brethren, my kinsmen according to the flesh.

ROMANS 9.3

1

Finding the Gap

I shall never forget the summer of 1968. The church carved that date deep in my memory by granting me an unusual privilege. After four years at a theological college and five in the traditional ministry, I was permitted – though somewhat reluctantly! – to become a 'worker-priest'. (The inverted commas are necessary since Methodist ministers are not usually described as priests.) I moved away from the centre of church life to a position which, to the casual glance, must have seemed almost peripheral. I became a bus driver. Within an ecumenical team ministry, I continued to preach and celebrate the sacraments, but I was dependent financially upon my secular employment.

The years passed with amazing swiftness. In 1988 I had the unexpected joy of being called to civic office, and was elected Sheriff of the city where I had worked for twenty years as 'the bus-driver/minister'. I was moved by this honour and saw in it a kind of vindication, both of my original determination to reach outside the confines of ordained ministry as normally understood, and of my church's generosity in giving me my head. I wore a cassock at every civic engagement – and there were over five hundred – as a deliberate and continuing act of witness. I felt I was repaying, in part, my debt to a church which had invested in me heavily and received little traditional ministry in return.

I cannot deny that – in many respects – the church backed a loser when it selected me for its ministry. I have felt mildly guilty about it from the outset. I served in two circuits, for a total of just five years. The simple truth is

that my ministry was sabotaged and thoroughly under-
mined before it had ever really begun. Looking back, I can
pinpoint the exact moment. It was a sunny Sunday afternoon. I was half-way through my college course, and it
was during the summer vacation. I was cycling back from
taking a service at a chapel which has long since been
demolished, and had almost reached home. I was twenty-
one, newly married, and wearing a dog-collar. As I turned
into the road on the council estate where I lived, I passed a
crowd of youths sprawled out on the grass verge, playing
cards. I heard one remark, loudly: 'There goes one of
them dirty old vicars!' I grinned, but was inclined otherwise to ignore the comment. Then suddenly, on impulse, I
braked, turned round, and rode back to ask for clarifica-
tion. None was forthcoming. That round, at least, went to
me. But what I could never have guessed at the time was
how this chance encounter was to influence the shape of
the ministry for which I was still being trained.

My wife, Molly, and I grew to know those teenagers –
they were not *much* younger than us – and they came to
regard our home as their headquarters and regular
meeting-place. Over the two years which followed, they
made an impact upon me which has never faded. They
accepted me as an equal; they were intrigued by my calling; they would question eagerly and discuss endlessly.
But they didn't go to church. The possibility never
occurred to them. Yet whenever I had to leave them to
return to college for a few weeks, the culture shock was
almost unbearable. It was those youngsters, in the early
1960s, who introduced me to 'the gap' – who, in their
persons, directed me, with stark and undeniable clarity, to
the enormous gulf which existed between their lives and
all things ecclesiastical.

This gulf was not simply between the church and the
council estate residents. That was merely one of its more

dramatic manifestations. The gulf was far, far wider. And even at that early date, it dawned upon me that it would take more than new translations and 'modernised' services to bridge it. I shall examine the nature of 'the gap' in due course. Indeed, it is the underlying concern behind everything contained in these pages. But for the moment, I record simply that the direction of my entire ministry was determined in that split second when a cheeky teenager shouted to me in the street, and I seized the moment as an opportunity. Thirty years later he still has no time for religion, but we remain friends; something good came out of our encounter! Throughout those years, I neither forgot, nor amended, the lessons which my gang of youngsters taught me. They had taken me to the edge of the gap, and helped me to step warily across. They had shared their thoughts and feelings with me, and encouraged me to understand. They set in motion the chain of events which led to my long period of ministry as a worker-priest.

Not once have I regretted my years as a bus driver, for the gap still exists – if anything, wider than ever. As a worker-priest I have straddled two worlds, perfectly at home in both – and in neither. I have attempted to justify my pattern of ministry by asserting it to be in harmony with, and an expression of, the doctrine of Creation, the Incarnation, and the life and ministry of our Lord. Again, these are themes which recur later. They are central to any consideration of the gap and its implications for the church today.

At the end of a long interview during my shrievalty, a shrewd reporter surprised me by asking what twenty years as a worker-priest had done *to me*, and what I had derived personally from the venture. I deflected the question, not because I resented it but because I was immediately interested, and wanted to give it the consideration it merited. I'm still not entirely sure of the answer, although a few

things have become clear. First, I have enjoyed the cama-
raderie of the bus-workers and the laughter, the banter,
and the blunt exchanges of the canteen. I am, now, even
more reluctant to separate sheep from goats, and not even
sure to which group I myself belong!

Second, I have become hardened by shift work – not
physically, particularly, but inwardly. Squeezing between
closely-parked vehicles with an icy watering-can in the
blackness of a cold and windy winter morning, long before
daybreak, eventually breeds a distinctly no-nonsense approach to life. Hours spent in rush-hour traffic somehow
reinforces that tendency. So does walking home through
the city streets after midnight, following a late shift; or
chairing a noisy trade union branch meeting; or driving a
double-decker in fog, or in snow. It's not easy to convey
exactly what I mean, but I sense it is important to try. I am
confessing that experiences like those I have described
(and many others, including being sworn at regularly),
gradually sent me home 'tougher' than I was before; and
this 'toughness' affected my ecclesiastical perspective.
Less and less of traditional church life seemed really to
matter; more and more the church appeared to resemble a
club for those who happened to like that kind of thing.
Then, one day, I remembered that I had noticed this kind
of hardness in my council estate youngsters: a form of
maturity I had found instructive to contrast with the ethos
of life in a theological college. Now it had happened to me.

Third, my catholicity increased: my sympathies broad-
ened, my interests widened. The sense of being cut off
from the daily life of the world, and trapped in the church
– against which I fought during the first years of my ministry – vanished immediately I became a worker-priest,
and never returned. Sacred and secular merged to
become equally valid sources of revelation. As I learned
to discern the same Spirit at work in both, the whole

universe – buses and Bibles – became exciting and inviting and meaningful.

Fourth, I have developed what I can only describe as a form of detachment. (Bus driving is ideally suited to the study of human nature!) I don't mean that my commitment to the gospel has become half-hearted or lukewarm. I mean that, frequently, I have a curious sense of being a watcher or an observer – even when I am a participant. Now, whenever I think about the church, it is from a position which – while certainly not outside – is decidedly on the fringe emotionally. I fear I have not explained my stance very clearly; nevertheless that is the vantage-point from which I have written these pages, and I hope the way I feel will become plain in due course.

When I embarked upon a worker-priest ministry it was in the full knowledge that no safety-nets were strung beneath me. Of course, if things had gone disastrously wrong the church would probably have rescued me and found, eventually, a place for me again in the traditional work. That, I must admit ungratefully, was no consolation. It was part of the problem. It was a powerful spur to persevere. I had lost my faith in 'the system'. Young and inexperienced as I was, it had broken my heart. I no longer believed it was geared to the needs of the gospel in modern Britain. But I felt that my experiment was *real*. There was to be no stipend, no expenses, no house provided. I wanted to be a twentieth-century evangelist.

Not many people shared my vision. I found that women were generally more sympathetic than men, younger people seemed to understand better than older people, and those outside the church grasped the idea more easily, by far, than those inside.

But because the venture was real, the risks were real, too. I was no shy school-leaver, to be excused endless mistakes and indiscretions. I was an ordained minister of religion deliberately opting to infiltrate a situation in which committed Christians were not numerous, and I was determined to stay there, with no preconceived strategy, to see what would happen. I was exposed and vulnerable. In religious language, I was risking the loss of heaven in being prepared to journey towards hell, towards places where the Divine Love is prevented from shining brightly – and all in the hope of throwing a bridge across the gap. I could have lost my faith within a fortnight; I could, through inexperience, have been involved in a serious accident; I could easily have become embroiled in debt, for I had no money; I could have fallen into serious moral disarray. Those were some of the more obvious risks which had to be taken if my 'experiment' was to be authentic. If I entertained serious hopes of touching lives which were light years away from the influence of the church, a willingness to face such disturbing possibilities was the price I had to pay. For the sake of the gospel, I paid. And I survived. But I have not escaped unscathed. By crossing the gap and spending most of my waking hours there, I earned, eventually, the right to bear my own peculiar witness to the Love which, I believe, lies at the heart of all things. But genuine 'meeting' is a two-way phenomenon; it involves giving *and* receiving – for better or worse. So be prepared!

In these chapters I propose to look, first, at the doctrines of the church, and then to examine its three primary activities: evangelism, service to the community, and worship. Then I wish to discuss the importance of 'folk religion'. My concern, throughout, will be to illustrate the gap between the church and the ordinary non-churchgoer, and to ask if anything can be done about it. These thoughts and emotions have been heavily influenced by my years spent on the road and in a bus garage, with the smell of hot tyres and diesel for incense. I have become a kind of reverend outsider.

I hope, therefore, that nobody will picture this book being written in church (though I am in church daily). Imagine, instead, a figure in a uniform with a peaked cap, tapping on the window of the church, mouthing, gesticulating, and trying with difficulty to make himself understood.

2

The Mystery, the Tenderness and the Power

Not many of the people with whom I work find much time for organised religion. When the subject arises, however, several will always conclude: 'I think there must be *something* there . . .' Others are not so sure. One driver said recently, inelegantly but with great emphasis: 'We don't know *nothing*. We *can't* know . . .' I have, temperamentally, great sympathy with that viewpoint, and regard it as a refreshing mark of humility rather than a culpable lack of 'faith'. Some brands of religious certainty strike me as utterly false, profoundly embarrassing, and arrogant in the extreme. When confronted by them I recoil instantly, and flee, in spirit, back to the comparative sanity of the canteen. Religion and mystery are inextricably entwined. In religious discussion I certainly do not ask for deliberate obscurity; neither do I exalt ignorance above sound learning and personal experience. But I look for the humble, tentative reverence which becomes the creature contemplating its Origin.

Each busy working day I marvel at the sheer number of people who throng the city streets, jostling shoulder to shoulder, sometimes stepping dangerously from the pavement, uncomfortably close to my bus. Those lives are all interlinked – yet each has a unique identity, each is a separate world. This individual awareness of self-consciousness which we call 'life' is an experience none of us asked for, and it is frankly difficult to make head or tail of it. There are no boundaries, no fixed points of reference. Everything is moving, changing, becoming; distinctions are blurred, and conclusions provisional; rigid definitions are usually unrealistic, often inaccurate, and invariably misleading. The concepts of space and time provide the most obvious examples. We can measure *so far*, but eventually our calculations become less meaningful. We know we inhabit planet Earth, whose position in the cosmos we can describe in relation to the sun and the other known stars; but what lies beyond the black, unimaginable distances of outer space defies our comprehension. In a similar way, historical periods of time are difficult enough for most of us to appreciate: geological time and astronomical time are almost impossible for creatures destined to enjoy only three score years and ten. There is always a 'beyond'; and our understanding and measuring of time and space is ultimately arbitrary and relative.

I am interested when my unbelieving friends scorn the religious concept of 'eternity'. Because we live in fragile, exquisite little bodies wonderfully fashioned out of mud – with our personal history compressed between the dates of our birth and death – it is hard for us to own the possibility of existence without beginning and without end. It is outside our experience. Yet the notion of eternity seems, to me, to present no problems greater than those inherent in the concepts of time and space.

So we don't really know where we are, and we're unsure of the time. To make matters worse, we don't know what we're made of. Our bodies, intriguing shapes and sensations, are formed of chemicals, which are composed of elements, which are constructed from atoms, which are, in turn, made up of whatever it is which finally constitutes matter. Matter, we are told, is energy mysteriously concentrated. And energy . . .? Again, we search in vain for a starting-point. I know it is twenty miles from my house to the coast; that I am writing this on 4th December; that my body needs at least one good meal a day. But beyond these elemental discoveries are profound mysteries of space and time and matter, capable of teasing and tantalising the thoughtful mind throughout a lifetime. (And, contrary to my expectations as a young man, the mysteries increase and intensify – rather than diminish – as the years pass.)

And that is only the beginning. This awareness that we exist suspended in mystery leads quickly to a realisation that most of the other decisive factors which fashion our nature and destiny are similarly fluid, and defy the application of sharp dividing lines. For example, if humankind has evolved from the lower animals – a beautiful hypothesis which gives us kinship with all the creatures – the transition was gradual. We did not suddenly assume our present form (and instantly become lovable) one particular Wednesday afternoon.

A variation on the same theme is contained in the battles which rage over the abortion issue. When does human life begin? When is a foetus 'viable'? Those whose conclusions differ are, nonetheless, able to present strong and cogent arguments. Is it here? Is it there? Or is it somewhere in between? Human sexuality provides another illustration in the fact that – physical differences notwithstanding – our sexuality is most accurately represented as a spectrum upon which we all appear, but with 'male' and 'female' characteristics mixed, to varying degrees, in us all.

Indeed, our very characters are themselves alarmingly variable. We can seem to be different people at different times: different – morning, midday, and evening; different – as life moves through its various stages; different – depending upon the weather, illness, companions, and all life's endlessly changing circumstances. And where does genuis end and insanity begin? The line between those who manage to cope with life and those who fail is exceedingly fine, and forever moving. Even religious conversion, for most people, is a process. At which point does the bud become a tulip? It doesn't suddenly open: the colour seeps slowly and wonderfully into it.

Most of us realise that the decisions and choices we have to make are usually varying shades of grey. That principle can be detected, in some form or another, in every area of life. Nothing is fixed. Continents move; coastlines alter; infants gradually become pensioners. Again, is it *really* possible to identify and distinguish between saints and sinners? I find saintliness and sinfulness are usually jumbled up together. But now I am leaping ahead. For the moment, at the risk of labouring the point, I am trying to support Eric, who swears like a trooper yet perceives something many Christians overlook. When he declares, 'We don't know . . . we *can't* know . . .' he is correctly drawing attention to a basic and fundamental element which any religion worth the name must include in its embrace.

Through the church window, I am trying to suggest that the unrequested experience of life with which we have been saddled is not unlike one of those Christmas games which promise 'hours of fun for all the family', but which frequently leave everyone bewildered, confused, and slightly bad-tempered. How disturbingly *live* it all seems – with no second chances. And how brief! Even as we search for meaning it is passing quickly, accelerating towards another alarming unknown. We get one attempt only. There are no trial runs, and no rule books. There are no boundaries, no fixed points of reference. There is only *you*; and *now*; and *The Mystery*.

I hope, and believe, that the Christian doctrine of God is about The Mystery – the mystery of existence, the mystery of creation, the mystery of life and death, the mystery of love. It is here, however, that many non-churchgoers part from us. They are not unmindful of The Mystery, but they cannot relate it to our 'God'. They leave the matter open. They cannot believe in God in any definite sense, and with commendable honesty, they say so. The pity of it, however, is that they never penetrate beyond this particular philosophical concept (to which there is no final answer, other than the answers of faith and experience), to the other great insights of the Christian tradition.

I wish they could find an incentive to break this impasse and deliberately put their twentieth-century disbelief in abeyance for a while. It would be a perfectly honourable attitude to adopt. No one has seen God at any time. Perhaps He's there, perhaps He isn't. But if they could tacitly 'pretend' to believe – just to make us happy! – they would be free to concentrate on some of the chief features of the gospel which, in turn, shed gleams of light upon The Mystery. Something of this nature happens each year when a few of my workmates 'support me' by attending midnight mass on Christmas Eve – and surprise themselves by 'enjoying' it.

By the same token, I could wish for a keener acknowledgement, among many Christians, of the awesome and terrible mystery which lies behind our doctrine of God. I would like to feel it in our worship; I would like to sense it in our attitudes and conversation. I go cold inside when I hear people talking about God with breathtaking familiarity, and professing a detailed knowledge of the divine strategy. They have Him taped, and neatly tied up, and perfectly under control. Could anything be less real, or more laughable? The Mystery is Burning Light and Consuming Fire. Our clearest insights are but the palest reflections. To strut before The Mystery is folly.

As we think about God and the gap, I ask for a seemly and maximum sense of reverence and awe in our attitudes. A strong, quiet confidence in God is essential; but a cocksure familiarity with The Ultimate is unconvincing and embarrassing.

'But, surely, in the Bible it says . . .' an earnest church-man might interject; and I would immediately take guard. For the Bible says lots of things, and nothing causes me greater pain than the implication, frequently made, that the Scriptures – which all Christians love and revere – can only be handled in one fashion, constitute a collection of proof texts, and provide the final, fully-polished word on every moral and philosophical topic to which our restless, questioning minds can turn. If you personally find some form of fundamentalist approach to Scripture credible and devotionally helpful, we shall hold much ground in com-mon. We shall never fall out unless, or until, you imply that yours is the only true approach. I, myself, find a fun-damentalist attitude to the Bible unhelpful and unrealistic. The production of a string of biblical quotations *alone* has never convinced me of anything. Yet I refuse to surrender the Scriptures to those whose interpretations differ from my own.

I claim that my approach to the life-giving Scriptures has a validity equal to that of those who incline towards fundamentalism, and I utterly refuse to be put in the dock by them, or thrown perpetually on the defensive. *It is not necessary to be a fundamentalist to place the Scriptures at the centre of your devotional life.* On the contrary, idolatry can take many forms, and bibliolatry is one of them. All of us have favourite texts. 'Thy Word is a lamp unto my feet and a light unto my path' is one of mine. 'The letter kil-leth, but the spirit giveth life' is another. The new life in the Spirit, free and exciting, which catching a glimpse of the truth revealed in Jesus kindles, is nourished and guided by the Scriptures; but it is not weighed down, nor rigorously, minutely regulated by the Scriptures. Indeed, certain approaches to the Bible can produce harsh, unlov-ing, exclusive, self-righteous attitudes which run counter to everything for which the gospel stands. The spirit of the gospel must not be vitiated by our handling of the Scriptures.

In William Golding's *Free Fall*, young Johnny Spragg is caught day-dreaming during Miss Massey's Scripture lesson. He has been staring out of the window, watching an aeroplane soaring high among the clouds over Kent, and is completely at a loss when she questions him:

> 'Why did I tell you those three stories?'
>
> We could just hear his muttered answer. The Moth had flown away.
>
> 'Idunnomiss.'
>
> Miss Massey hit him on both sides of the head, precisely with either hand, a word and a blow.
>
> 'God –'
> Smack!
> '– is –'
> Smack!
> '– love!'
> Smack! Smack! Smack!
> You knew where you were with Miss Massey.

The basic Christian message of Divine Love can be easily blurred, but nothing distorts it more than a narrow, 'the-Bible-says' approach to Holy Scripture. The Bible frequently drops beneath its own high points, but it is the lofty peaks of its revelation – the essential message of a wonderful Love – that interest me, primarily; not the watermarks on the envelope in which the message was delivered. The Book we treasure most did not fall, completed, into our hands from the sky. It was compiled by people seeking after God, searching for meaning amid the mystery.

But while the Bible is precious to churchgoers, on the other side of the gap ignorance of the Scriptures is fast becoming total. There remains, among a few, a little

14

dangerous knowlege. Sayings like 'An eye for an eye, and a tooth for a tooth' are quoted from time to time, but not with understanding. I have a little talk about the Bible which I've delivered over a cup of tea in the canteen more times than I can remember. Its simple outline runs as follows:

1. The Bible is not just one book, but a collection of sixty-six books . . .
2. It was not written by one person but by a great number . . .
3. It was not written at one long sitting, but over a period of hundreds of years . . .
4. It contains examples of almost every type of literature imaginable – and this fact has to be kept constantly in mind when its message is read. It contains myth, legend, history, law, fiction, songs, poetry, proverbs, prophecy, apocalyptic, manifesto, diary, travel, romance, letters, and gospels.
5. The link which joins these separate strands together is the theme of God's self-revelation . . .
6. It is a *progressive* revelation, which reaches a climax in the Cross, but continues still . . .

My advice is always the same: 'Read the Bible carefully; capture its unmistakable spirit; then go back and read it again, interpreting its words in the light of its own spirit.' I have come to realise that my little talk is needed in church today, nearly as urgently as in the canteen . . . However, the Bible is now largely confined, like a threatened species, to the church side of the gap; and the gap is wide. If it is to be closed, it will not be by building a bridge of Bibles across. Things have gone too far.

Yet looking from the bus garage, across the gap, towards the church, two great, related, Bible themes shine with exciting brilliance: the doctrine of Creation and the doctrine of the Incarnation. Both testify to the unity of God's church and God's world. God is the Creator of all things, and His creation is good. 'All things were made by him . . . And the Word was made flesh, and dwelt among us.' The Creator was not ashamed to become intimately and uniquely part of his own creation, for ever binding together 'sacred' and 'secular': for ever hallowing all things physical, particularly our bodies; for ever asserting that each weekday is as 'holy' as Sunday; for ever insisting that the Divine is as active and as likely to be encountered in society (in its history, organisations, movements, and events) as in the life of the church; for ever branding attempts to save people from the 'world' as a nonsense, doomed to failure.

To share this biblical revelation of a God whose unrestricted sphere of activity embraces the whole world, with all its agony and hope; and to share, too, the realisation that we meet God – the Ultimate, the Mysterious – most directly *in one another* (and especially in the poor), is an intensely liberating experience. God is not locked in the vestry; neither has He gone off to Synod for the day. He upholds the entire creation moment by moment, and speaks to us out of the struggles, the achievements, the sufferings, and the loving relationships of his people – *all* his people. The church has a special place in God's affections and a particular role and function in the diving economy; but it has no monopoly of the Divine Spirit. 'The wind bloweth where it listeth.' Tenderness, laughter, incongruity, beauty, pain and pathos are everywhere, and we are compelled to respond to their impact. I have often felt that if you cannot see God in the Larkin novels of H.E. Bates, or in Gilbert and Sullivan, or on 'News at Ten', you are unlikely to find Him in the church or in the Bible.

Peering in through the Gothic windows, however, I see precious truths embodied in the doctrines of the church, the lustre and value of which are enhanced by the gloom which envelops so much of God's world: 'The light shineth in the darkness.' Someone might be tempted to ask: 'If God is active on both sides of the gap, does it really matter if the gap is bridged or not?' It matters to *both* sides. Christianity will not flourish in an enclosed, refined, and artificial 'religious' atmosphere. The end-product will not be the real thing. Christianity *belongs* in the world, and thrives on the raw materials of everyday life.

In the pub and in the garage, I am not ashamed of the gospel. The Christian message is capable of being interpreted in various ways. It retains a powerful and distinctive ability to illustrate the human condition and influence it for good. Those who are unfamiliar with its incisive and beneficial stimulus are missing out. Its insights are timeless, pertinent, and a source of hope and encouragement to those who know where to look.

Here is an example of the way in which the world and the gospel provide a commentary on each other. Many years ago I had a friend who left his wife (of whom I was equally fond). I did everything possible to avert this tragedy, but without success. The story eventually had a happy ending, but in those sad and depressing weeks I saw many of the deepest truths of the gospel enacted with a clarity and intensity that shook me to the core.

The girl was crucified. Her love was thrown back in her face. She plumbed the depths of rejection – the hellish desolation of 'My God, my God, why hast thou forsaken me?' I saw what sin does to love. I shared in the cost of attempting to reconcile – and significantly, one of the most terrible days was a Good Friday. It affected, permanently, my understanding of Holy Week. I caught a glimpse of what Good Friday means, and it nearly destroyed me. I was utterly torn, utterly drained. Sermons about crucifixion can easily sound technical, clinical, cerebral; but to be involved in any act of reconciliation is to approach the awesome mystery of atonement.

All Christian theories of the Atonement no doubt reflect facets of the truth, however crude and inadequate they may sometimes sound. But the basic fact is inescapable. There *is* a price to pay in any act of reconciliation. The doctrine of the Atonement is not preached by the church to keep the theologians occupied; it is there because it embodies cosmic realities.

I stood between them, and shared their suffering. I thought of the psalmist: 'For it cost more to redeem their souls . . .' I thought of the old Sankey hymn:

> But none of the ransomed ever knew
> How deep were the waters crossed,
> Nor how dark was the night that the Lord passed
> through . . .

They never knew. Exhausted and spent, I could have groaned: 'I thirst.' And, all the time, that terrible ache inside . . .

These insights into love and pain and suffering and atonement became almost too awesome to endure. I could not switch off my love for him, but I could not condone; nor could I suddenly, and without reason, forsake her, at the time of her most desperate need. Some decisions became inevitable. The fundamental decision, from which I shrank – 'Let this cup pass from me' – could finally be avoided no longer. So, because I loved him, I had to give him up. I don't mean I refused to talk to him; still less that I stopped liking him. But I accepted that things could never again be the same; the foundations of our relationship had shifted, and were now fatally flawed. We both knew it.

I could have decided differently – as part of me wanted, more than anything else in the world. It was a friendship that meant a great deal to me. I could have made excuses for him. It was an insidious and powerful temptation. A voice whispered: 'Side with him. Why should *you* suffer? This doesn't concern you. Despite this upheaval, your friendship can be salvaged.' I wavered, and then recovered. To have heeded the voice would have been to betray him with a kiss. Friendship and love have to include honesty and respect. But the temptation was great.

I did not 'abandon' him because I no longer loved him. I loved him so much that I was prepared to sacrifice the bond between us rather than cheapen it by placing it on an unworthy footing, pretending that everything was all right and unaltered when it was not. So I saw him less; and, when we met, the carefree sense of fun had been replaced by a hesitancy, a seriousness, a guarded, defensive stance, as if an unspoken question lay between us.

I could easily understand somebody else being led to a different conclusion. I did what I had to do, yet it brought me little peace. I felt I had deserted him. Would not a *true* friend have stood beside him, regardless of every circumstance, and shared, if necessary, his dishonour and disgrace? These are profound matters, and not a stone's throw from the Cross of Christ. In the gospel story, Christ stands by *us* in our sin and shame . . . and God loved Him so much He let Him die rather than distort his revelation of Love . . .

Crucifixion and Atonement! These are doctrines which belong in the bus garage as well as the church. Their significance is not narrowly 'religious'; it is universal and cosmic.

One tiny detail which I noticed filled me with curiosity and awe. After the first shock had been assimilated, the girl assumed a new, quiet dignity. But more than that – and I find this difficult to define precisely – she looked beautiful. Hurt and humiliated, abandoned and resigned,

her future in ruins, she looked stunningly beautiful . . .
The fascination of the Cross; the beauty of the Crucified
. . . Then I became more powerfully aware of 'the sinfulness of sin'; of the dark forces which could do this terrible
thing. 'The heart is deceitful above all things and desperately wicked.'

Later came the agonising realisations: 'What have I done
to her?' 'What have I done to myself?' 'Can it ever be put
right?' 'How?' 'And when he came to himself, he said . . .'

But when those early longings for reconciliation began
to stir, pride initially prevented the first uncertain steps
towards home from being taken. How true the slogan we
teach the children: 'I' is at the centre of sIn and at the
heart of prIde!

Then matters developed astonishingly fast. A few weeks
earlier, all warm, affectionate feelings had gone, he
claimed. The will to try again had gone. The relationship
was dead. But new strength, new determination, new
warmth, and new feelings arose – on both sides. The dead
bones of the marriage began to live – and Christian doctrine was enacted again, before my very eyes. When new
attitudes dawn where previously there existed only dry-
ness, barrenness, and hopelessness, *there the Holy Spirit is
at work*.

I have given instructions that, should ever I start speaking in tongues, I must be taken home, put straight to bed,
and my GP contacted immediately. And, for goodness
sake, don't tell them at work! There is nothing dis-
tinctively Christian about speaking in tongues. It is a phenomenon linked with certain mental attitudes and
emotional conditions, and has been manifested in seers,
dervishes, and religious devotees of all ages and cultures. I
heard it described, recently, as possessing little spiritual
significance – no more than any other involuntary bodily
noise. Despite its wide impact, I do not look to the charis-

matic movement as the force to bridge the gap. My under-standing of the Holy Spirit doesn't stretch far in that dir-ection – though I'm beginning to feel in a minority. But when I see tired, or defeated, or hopeless men and women filled with new energy, new ideals, new determination, and new love, 'I believe in the Holy Ghost, the Lord and Giver of Life.'

Finally, to my friends came the forgiveness, the accept-ance, the thankfulness for a fresh start, the new commit-ment, and the new intentions. We had passed from crucifixion to resurrection. The new relationship was so tender and joyful that one *almost* dared to wonder whether the pain had not been worth enduring, in order to create such love. To that question there is no answer. It is part of the mystery.

Resurrection is the theme which lies at the heart of the gospel, and it possesses immense contemporary signifi-cance. Again, I turn to a Sankey hymn – the music-hall numbers among Christian hymnody – to express this truth with directness and simplicity:

> Down in the human heart, crushed by the tempter,
>   Feelings lie buried that grace can restore:
> Touched by a loving hand, wakened by kindness,
>   Chords that were broken will vibrate once more.

In the lives of most people, many little deaths have taken place. Talents have been neglected, and have shrivelled and perished. Gifts have been squandered; ideals have been crushed by disillusionment; tenderness has been mocked, gentleness scorned, warmth rejected. Love is crucified daily in a black mystery which parallels the rejec-tion of Jesus, the Man of Sorrows, who healed the multi-tudes but who, at the last, was acquainted with grief. But as the experience of my friends testifies, crucifixion can lead to resurrection. That is not a religious insight alone. It

is a spiritual, emotional, psychological insight of great
value. An unexpected new development; a word of encouragement; a bit of practical support; some genuine
friendship; some time and care and attention – then, shyly
at first, but with ever-increasing confidence, 'Chords that
were broken will vibrate once more.'

When lives appear shattered beyond hope of repair;
when people have been abandoned, or tricked, or abused;
when, in the very darkest hours, death itself occasionally
seems more welcoming than the lonely, empty, endless
hours of hurt, and the gnawing pain of rejection, and the
inexplicable absence of a familiar and much-loved body,
crucifixion is a hideous reality. The state of desolation,
when love is gone, is hell. Pain like that can destroy. *Yet it
need not.* If we can find and accept some help; if we can
muster the determination and courage to hang on, day by
day, night after long night; then, despite the pain and the
tears, new things begin to grow in the desert of our grief
and despair. Sometimes new relationships are formed,
new plans are made, new and satisfying routines evolve.
Sometimes old relationships, which seemed dead, come
miraculously to life, reborn, renewed, resurrected, burning with an intensity even more wonderful than before.
The bitter experiences leave scars. The Risen Christ bore
scars. But they were glorious scars testifying to the ultimate victory of Love – the power for which no word is
adequate, but which Christians believe upholds, from
moment to moment, the whole creation.

Resurrection is the doctrine which expresses Christian
faith in the inevitable and final victory of light over darkness, knowledge over ignorance, health and healing over
disease and suffering, peace over war, love over hatred,
good over evil, life over death. It is not only about church,
Sunday, Easter, and the hereafter. It is about the possibilities inherent in all human relationships. It is the gospel

for the bus garage; and for the coal mine, the office block, and the boardroom. When two old friends quarrel bitterly, but eventually are reconciled and resume their friendship, a small miracle of resurrection has taken place.

I wish, therefore, that my workmates and my many non-churchgoing friends could summon the time and the inclination to think more deeply about the Christian religion, and to participate, occasionally, in a religious rite. This is not because I'm anxious to boost congregations and collections, but for reasons far more important. Religion provides a language for the interpretation of areas of experience which tend, otherwise, to remain largely unexamined. It provides models and a framework of ideas within which moral and philosophical concepts can be explored. Crucifixion, atonement, resurrection, sin, confession, repentence, forgiveness, the Holy Spirit, priesthood, prayer – all these, and more, found reflection in the story of separation and reconciliation I told. I have called them cosmic themes because they are rooted and grounded and woven into the very fabric of creation, and apply to believers and unbelievers alike.

Whenever I am able to share Christian insights with people on the other side of the gap, even at what many would regard as this elementary, demythologised, or symbolic level, I am more than glad. The language of our Christian sub-culture has become so foreign to them that any small breakthrough in communication is a step forward. In any case, the gospel is 'true' at various and different levels. The God of the Christians is at large, and not restricted within the confines of any religious tradition. The whole creation is upheld by His Spirit and subject to His rule. All the great biblical themes, therefore, are capable of the widest application. I *long* for people to participate regularly in worship, to make acts of commitment, and to enjoy deep spiritual experiences. But this, at least, is a *start*, and can lead to those more profound insights for which, I believe, the souls of men and women are hungering as urgently as ever. 'Thou hast made us for thyself, and our hearts are restless until they find their rest in thee.'

The most precious insights of all are those which reflect the truth which forms the very pinnacle of New Testament revelation. Christianity is about Love. It is about the warmth and compassion, tenderness and self-sacrifice, gentleness and lowly service we recognise in the life of Christ – and which, somehow, demand a verdict from us. The words of Jesus have an authority we can either accept or reject, but cannot deny. He tells us things which, deep down, we have always known; and He says that – if we want – we can share the same spirit and the same quality of life we have recognised in Him. Christianity is also about straight dealing, and justice, and peace, and righteousness, in personal and social affairs. That's Love, too – as we shall see.

Christianity is not about cleverness. Intellectual brilliance fills me with awe, and rather frightens me. I'm afraid that my beliefs, or lack of them, will be held up for examination, and that I shall be scorned if I am unable adequately to defend them. Fancy feeling like that! We should certainly develop, to the full, the abilities we have been given, intellectual or otherwise. But Christianity is about *love*: and in that realm, an unlettered old woman from the country or the slums can easily be greater in the Kingdom of God than a university professor. The test is never 'How clever am I?' but 'How loving?' That comforting thought has another side to it, however, which is sobering to contemplate. If we are out-loved by those who do not hope in Christ, our discipleship is called seriously into question.

Looking in from outside at our doctrines, I still rejoice at what I see. I see Jesus, who thrills and attracts. The church's teaching that His life of love reflects the essential nature of the creation, teases and overwhelms. The Cosmic Christ! The Kingdom of which He spoke will feature prominently in a subsequent chapter. We have something good to share! We have a gospel worth proclaiming!

The doctrine of the Holy Trinity summarises much of what I have tried to suggest in this chapter. Christianity is not a Jesus sect, although Jesus is utterly central to Christian devotion and discipleship. The Christian religion rests upon the doctrine of the Holy and Undivided Trinity, and Trinity Sunday – far from being an embarrassment – is, properly understood, the crown of the Christian year. The doctrine of the Holy Trinity is about The Mystery – The Mystery revealed yet always beyond, always beckoning. It is about Unity in Diversity, and Diversity in Unity – like life itself. It binds together the different expressions of our faith; the awe and the majesty and the mystery; the compassion which offers a cup of water, and the tenderness which offers a kiss; and the energy, the power, and the reborn will. Above all, it asserts something which is overwhelming in its simplicity and daring: The Mystery is Love.

> The Father shining on His throne,
> The glorious co-eternal Son,
>   The Spirit, one and seven,
> Conspire our rapture to complete;
> And lo! we fall before His feet,
>   And silence heightens heaven.

3

Called to be Evangelists

A searing awareness of the gulf which exists between the church and the majority of our fellow-countrymen has haunted my ministry. I may, of course, be wrong about it. The gap may be much narrower than I imagine; or it may not exist at all. Perhaps it is a projection of my own inner turmoil, and everything in the garden is lovely. Sadly, too much evidence points the other way. There is a deepening cultural divide between those of us who feel at home in public worship and are familiar with the vocabulary, and those who have lost the church-going habit, or have never possessed it. This divide cuts across social divisions, and affects the well-off and well-educated just as much as everyone else. However, it is undeniably among those who once were described as the working classes that the alienation from organised religion is most obvious and complete.

Is the gap as wide in rural as in urban areas? Thirty years ago I would have said, 'Probably not.' A residential, affectionate, intuitive recognition of the church's place in the scheme of things still lingered. It was not to linger unaltered much longer. That sentimental, historical legacy of respect for the church, coupled with a vague sense of belonging to it in some distant and undemanding way, has become further diluted in recent years. The social impact of television and the private car has not been confined to urban areas. There is as much modern sophistication, superficiality, and ruthless selfishness to be found in the villages as in the cities.

In many places, urban and rural, the work of the church is flourishing today, and we are all cheered when we hear stories of consolidation and advance. Often, the church is recognised as an integral and vital part of the community; its premises may be used by all kinds of organisations; perhaps even the congregations have increased. 'There's no great gulf *here*,' you protest – and I am glad, and pray that your work for God will continue to bring fulfilment to His people and honour to His Name.

So what, exactly, am I moaning about? I am restless and uneasy because, despite all the good things happening, I cannot shake off the spectre of the great divide. If it is hard to define precisely, its origins, at least, are no great mystery. The rapid advance of scientific knowledge; the carnage, upheaval, and disillusionment of world wars; vast social changes and new recreational opportunities; the church's historical tendency to side with the rich and the powerful – all these have contributed.

None of those boys playing cards on the green verge went to church. Only a handful of my present workmates have religous affiliations. Few local members of the political party to which I belong attend even civic religious events. Not many of my trade union branch officials have strong church links. Most of the regulars in my pub put church attendance low on their list of priorities. That is the environment in which I live. Those are the incontrovertible facts I have to face, daily. It is a far cry from the ethos of church meeting and public worship. Small wonder that when I have to attend ecclesiastical assemblies, I sometimes feel like a fish out of water!

Ministers of religion, as the officially accredited representatives of the church, cannot avoid being included in the scope of this discussion. Indeed, they are at the centre of it – and I want to ask a question. Why do some of the people who wear dog-collars, who inhabit the same planet as everyone else, read the same newspapers, use the same supermarkets, are involved in society at many points, and previously earned a living amid the hurly-burly of industry and commerce, seem slightly out of touch and ill at ease when surrounded by non-churchgoers? The question is asked in a brotherly spirit and with genuine bewilderment. Many will dismiss it as uncharitable nonsense. One half of me is inclined to agree and wants to withdraw the question – but the other half will not yield. I see a gap, which I do not believe to be part of God's plan, between the church and the world – and too many clergy are stranded on the wrong side.

Serving the church *can* be cosy. Any club or society has the potential to become a self-contained little world-within-a-world, and the church is no exception. Indeed, with its liturgy, its distinctive vocabulary and, above all, its theology (the source of its 'authority'), the tendency is greatly reinforced. The best place to hide from God is in church, among all the paraphernalia of religion. There's a good chance that He'll never find you there. And the sacred ministry provides the very best hiding-place of all.

Religious activities create a slipstream into which it is easy to get drawn in such a way that something basic and human is impaired, or even lost. There is a type of natural-ness, gaiety, spontaneity – almost a *worldliness* – which can easily be forfeited. When we allow this to happen, we have lost touch with Jesus. He is likely to startle us by reappear-ing suddenly, on the far side of the gap, relaxed, smiling, and utterly at home.

From the bus garage, ministers of religion are viewed with indifference. For the most part, paths never cross. Some-times clergy provoke a mild interest: 'I talked to the vicar at the reception. He seemed a decent sort of bloke.' Just occa-sionally a wistfulness creeps into a clerical encounter, and the unbeliever speaks earnestly and seriously, as if hoping we might have something useful to say. Unfortunately, we sel-dom rise to the occasion. When the crunch comes, we find ourselves anchored – emotionally, theologically, and economically – on the wrong side of that gap so tantalisingly difficult to demarcate, but so easy to sense and see.

The clerical contribution to the gap has a definite economic dimension. When a person becomes dependent financially upon the church, his attitude to religious matters and his entire relationship to the church are inevitably affected. This seldom operates at the crude level of fearing to offend the people who pay the wages – though such constraints, in one form or another, are not unknown. The damage is done at deeper and more subtle levels.

A ministerial friend was compelled to superannuate early for reasons of ill-health. Eventually, a partial recovery enabled him to return to his original, secular, profession. His joy and sense of fulfilment knew no bounds. I listened to him carefully, and we compared notes with unanimity. The simple satisfaction of knowing that wages had been earned in the market-place and not cobbled together with difficulty from a tight budget or from the gifts of former generations; the sense of being in touch; the thrill of being treated as an ordinary human being, receiving neither the deference (sometimes grudging, sometimes sincere), nor the suspicion and coolness which the cloth is prone to attract – all these had combined to produce, for us both, experiences uncomfortably close to liberation.

The mission of the church would be grossly impaired without a stipendiary ministry. It is biblical and it is essential. Nevertheless, it has developed unfortunate side-effects. It contributes to the isolation of the ministry from the mainstream of everyday life; it filters off the flavour of the factory, the garage, the shop, and the office; it protects, and acts as a buffer – not least against the rigours of the employment market. It guarantees the continuation of the work of God in good times and in bad – but the price paid is not always a small one.

However, the gulf is not merely – or chiefly – a clerical phenomenon. Would that the problem were so simple! It is far more serious than that. The church is composed mainly of ordinary citizens who, in their various ways, are active members of the community. I believe the church stands accused before God, facing one grave charge. We have failed to help one another to see the unity of all things. We have repressed, rather than developed, our innate catholicism. We have fostered, despite endless warnings, a spiritual climate in which it is fatally easy for people to compartmentalise their lives, and file their religion away neatly in a drawer of its own. Our commitment and our discipleship have not been of a quality sufficient to prevent this distortion of the gospel.

So – we have praised our 'personal Saviour', and forgotten the Christ who beheld the city, and wept over it. We have become wealthy, and learned to live with our wealth. We have carried our Bibles to church blissfully unaware that small kegs of gunpowder would have been safer burdens. We have, disastrously, allowed our understanding of sexuality to be shaped by our hypocrisy and dishonesty. The doctrine of the Creation and the doctrine of the Incarnation have not gripped our imagination, nor freed our vision of God from an exclusively ecclesiastical context. We have supported worthy causes with distinction, but not enough of us have felt called to offer political service, and leadership in the labour movement. The Holy Trinity, testifying to the mysterious wholeness of God and His creation, has become a source of doctrinal bewilderment rather than of inspiration. Loudly, we sing: 'Our God reigns'; and we *know* He reigns in the church. We're not so sure about the pub.

In this way, the noble faith of the catholic church has been neutered. As a result, thousands of Christians are able to rejoice that the church does much good work. In its fellowship, they find guidance, comfort, support and encouragement. But they acknowledge no direct links between their religion and their business activities, their political activities, or their sex life. They have made Christianity a retreat, rather than a springboard; one of life's compartments, among many others. And yawning gaps have appeared, in all directions. Evangelism means taking leaps from the church across those gaps, and landing in other areas of God's creation, bearing with us the message of Love.

I must admit that a curious paradox exists at the heart of my thinking about evangelism. I mustn't exaggerate it or get it out of proportion, but I have to recognise it. The problem can be stated very simply: I like people as they are! I take people as I find them, warts and all, and try to extend to them the kind of total acceptance which I myself have been grateful to receive.

I don't want to be forever 'changing' people. I don't want my meetings with them to have an ulterior motive: my friendships a means to an end, my conversation always loaded. On the contrary – when I perceive myself to be on the receiving end of any such approach, I resent it, and resist it, and become very sad. I remember a bus driver who was converted by the Jehovah's Witnesses, with whom he came into contact while operating for them a private hire. He took his new faith very much to heart. I liked the man, and enjoyed talking with him – but soon he began to bring *every* conversation round quickly to religion. Personally, I could endure that, since for me religion is a topic of endless fascination. But there was more to it. He was, in fact, 'pushing religion', as the phrase has it. He was questioning, hinting, criticising my personal views and faith, and urging and advocating the doctrines and claims of the Witnesses. He did this all the time, in every conversation, almost without exception. He was proselytising. I tried to be generous, and gave credit where it was due. He had the courage of his convictions; he took his faith seriously; he was, perhaps, an evangelist. But he had also become a bore; and, often, he was to be found sitting alone. He was not involved at the centre of the life of the garage (however that might be defined). He was not actively disliked – you couldn't dislike him. He was regarded, with some sadness, as ' a nice bloke who has been spoilt by religion'. He became almost friendless, and – a word I distrust but, in truth, it seems the right one – *irrelevant* to the situation in which God had placed him. He represented the antithesis of virtually everything for which I stood. I saw him as a warning: a warning against evangelism of the wrong kind.

A full-blooded doctrine of creation sees not merely its religious segments, but the whole of society – bus companies as well as church fellowships – as the sphere in which God is at work: the God who is Unity in Diversity, and Diversity in Unity. Wage claims and profits, friendships and hatreds, work and leisure, jokes and sympathy – with all the compromising, wholesome, sweaty, tender, dubious and satisfying situations which make up daily life – create situations which invite and require a response. It is in our reactions, our choices, our attitudes, our gestures, and our decisions, that the Spirit of the Living God is active.

In the snatches of conversation overheard as people pass us in the street; in the contents of our newspapers; in the unfolding of history; in laws and in Acts of Parliament; in the relationship between management and trade union in a work-place, year after year – assessments are being made, positions adopted, values acknowledged, standards appealed to, precedents set, justice administered, hopes nurtured, progress achieved, order established and visions pursued. For much of the time, we manage to keep the show (whatever it is) on the road. We find ways of living together, ways of discovering happiness and fulfilment. When we are unsuccessful, things go wrong: we fall out with cousin Rita, or go on strike, or go bankrupt, or go to prison, or go to war. Yet, either way, the process continues. Life goes on. Fresh decisions have to be made. And we insist on using those mysterious words like 'right', 'wrong' and 'ought', which beg so many questions.

Society itself is a kind of Bible; each person we meet, an encounter with the Divine. How exciting it is! Religion is not only about sacred rites. It is about everyday life and what we make of the challenges, the issues and the people that feature in its web of relationships and events. A fresh lesson about religion awaits us, new every morning.

'God saw every thing that he had made and behold it was very good.' God loves his creation, and all his creatures; and we are *all* his children. If that is not the bedrock of our gospel, I don't know what is. God is Love, and it is in Love that we live and move and have our being. It isn't a question of going to church and then God will love you. It isn't a question of 'doing' anything. God loved us before we were born. We are 'enveloped in love'. It is God's eternal attitude towards us. So, when we look at people, let not our first thought be to 'change' them. Let our first reaction be to *love* them – to offer openness, acceptance, warmth, friendship, compassion, vulnerability, and service. Let our second reaction be to *enjoy* them; they are God's handiwork, and in most wonderful ways reflect their Great Original.

This message of Divine Love has important implications which affect our approach to mission and evangelism. In particular, as we stare out across the gap, it puts some of our more casual thoughts about 'heaven' and 'hell' and 'salvation' into perspective. 'God loves you', we preach. 'He loves each one with a love that will not let you go; a love immense, unfathomed, unconfined; a love so strong and true that no power in this, or any other world, can weaken or destroy it!' That is the very heart and essence of the message we proclaim. That is our Good News.

What a pity when we spoil it, and make nonsense of it, by adding or implying: '*However*, if you do not respond; if you refuse to recognise this Love; if you do not come to church and get converted; if you die without assenting to the credal statements of the Christian Church – *you could be in serious trouble*. This wonderful, constant, inexhaustible, indestructible Love *will suddenly run out*! You will be lost!' Thus, at a stroke, we render our message null and void, make the gospel invalid, and make ourselves look silly.

We cannot have it both ways. Either God loves us all, saints and sinners, believers and unbelievers alike, with a Love which is eternal, or we are talking about a very different and lesser phenomenon – an attitude which can be turned off and on at will. And even 'human love', as we have seen, can do better than that. Love is terrible. It suffers; it endures the crucifixions we inflict upon each other; it wanders hopelessly through the hell of desolation which we enter when love is gone: but it does not, cannot, suddenly switch itself off.

But we had it right in the first place. Our message is Eternal Love. A positive response to love, of course, makes possible all kinds of exciting new relationships and developments which indifference to love, and unwillingness to love in return, can never allow. That is not the same as suggesting, however, that at a certain moment the Divine Love suddenly becomes the Divine Wrath. God loves us now, and He will love us for ever. His love to us is not a reward. It is His eternal nature. He is our Eternal Lover.

If we believe we may have gained a glimpse into the meaning behind The Mystery, we are under an obligation to share that insight with each generation struggling to make sense of human existence – in the same way that all other knowledge is passed on. Those who believe that this precious revelation is contained in the life of Christ, and concerns the Way of Love, have a duty to testify. This should always be done – remembering the immensity of The Mystery – in a humble spirit. 'Come and see' tends to cut more ice these days than 'Thus saith the Lord.'

'But where is the urgency in your outreach if you do not believe you are attempting to save souls which might otherwise be lost for ever?' some will ask. At this point, D.T. Niles' definition of evangelism as 'one beggar telling another where to find bread' is worth bearing in mind. The obligation to evangelise – to share the Good News – lies at the top of the church's agenda in every age. Its urgency is impossible to exaggerate, and nothing I have said about the universality of the Divine Love should be taken to imply otherwise.

There is an unmistakable note of crisis in the gospel, which bears equally upon both 'preacher' and hearer. It is the message of Advent: the day of His coming is eternally at hand. Tomorrow is not necessarily good enough. Some matters will undoubtedly be worked out in eternity; others must be settled now. How often we convince ourselves that life is about to change, and soon it will become easier to do the things we should already have been doing. When the children are a little older . . . when we've had our holiday . . . when we've paid all those bills . . . when we've moved house . . . *then* we'll make a start! It is an illusion. That ideal moment never comes. We should delay no longer. '*Today* if ye will hear his voice . . .' '*Now* is the accepted time . . .'

The gospel of the Love of God does two things. First, it sets a standard. It provides a guiding principle, and makes clear what our basic approach should be to the complex issues of human relationships, personal and social. (We differ in our judgements regarding the best ways of achieving particular goals, but that is the political small print, and a separate matter.) The standard, the principle, the basic approach is that embodied in the Sermon on the Mount and the parables of the Kingdom: the Love which cares, and puts the weakest first. That is the first thing the gospel does: it says, 'We were made to love one another, and our attitudes, our programmes, and our policies should reflect that principle.'

But the gospel of God's Love does more than that – and it is here that I have to fight strenuously to avoid sliding into the reassuring old words and comfortable thought-forms with which we in the church are all so happily familiar. The gospel diagnoses a fundamental flaw in human nature: a powerful tendency to act selfishly, which is a failure in love, and is called 'sin'. The gospel assures us that this condition can be righted, and we can be healed. It offers moral and spiritual resources – new power, new love – to overcome our weakness and deficiency. It says, to each one of us: 'You fail, repeatedly, to display loving attitudes in your relationships. You should; and you can.' Christ taught that we should love one another in the way that God loves us. The thrust of that teaching is both personal and social. It calls for loving personalities *and* loving policies.

All the great biblical themes illustrate the Love of God and highlight the pattern of the grain along which the life of the universe flows. They form a commentary on the cosmic principle of compassion. Sadly, much human activity cuts across the grain of the universe, with inevitable and tragic consequences. Health, peace and wholeness are lost; disharmony, disease and disunity flourish. Here the biblical mythology is particularly rich and powerful, and affects our approach to the task of evangelism.

Using the concepts, the words, and the framework of ideas which religion provides, I admit, unashamedly, that I believe in the doctrine of the Fall, and I believe in the doctrine of Original Sin. These notions repel me when poetic myth is paraded as history, and I am asked to calculate the probable location of the Garden of Eden; but as present realities, and as insights into the nature of humankind, these doctrines are of critical importance, and utterly central to our thinking on evangelism. Indeed, the story of Adam and Eve is, for me, one of the most meaningful and revealing in the Bible. It is not about the origin of sin. It is about the nature of sin – what it is like, and what it does: how it divides and separates and causes disharmony. And the drama of that story is re-enacted in the life of every man and woman.

Do you see the urgency creeping in? It is not the urgency of having to reach people before God's love turns to hate and he despatches them to hell. It is the urgency of knowing that lives are being lived at only half power: that vast areas of experience are being left undiscovered, undeveloped, and unexplored; that talents are lying dormant; that love is being stunted and denied; that sin and selfishness are eating away at what, otherwise, would be lives of stature and achievement; that men and women are contenting themselves with husks, when they might be drinking of the water of life, freely. That is the urgency.

It is not the urgency of having to haul people into the ship of salvation before they drown and are lost eternally. It is the urgency of equipping men and women to jump overboard, fired by the spirit of love and compassion, and – amid the waves and storms at the centre of God's world – to spend themselves in the service of the weak, the poor, the sorrowing, the neglected, the sick, the deprived, the tempted, and the forgotten ones, who are dying unreached and uncared for. There is the urgency.

It is the urgency of love. It brings us, again, to my paradox. Love shows itself in many wonderful ways, but in this context it often means simply an attitude of constant friendship, good will, good humour, vulnerability, kindness and warmth. Such love should flow from us as effortlessly as breathing. We should love people naturally and for their own sake, because they themselves are warm-hearted human beings, different, interesting, and with the same mix of vices and virtues that we possess.

That is the first half of the paradox. Each person is God's unique creation, God's unique window on the world, God's unique revelation, God's unique child. People can be tiresome. They can be despicable, and vile, and bloody-minded; but usually they are fun! Love can have no ulterior motive. It cannot be switched on and directed solely towards securing a person's conversion. If it is not unconditional it is not real. It has become something other than love. Love is a gentleness which wells up from secret, inner sources to touch and refresh those with whom we daily come into contact. They may not actually frame the words, but subconsciously they will recognise our sincerity and warmth, and respond by displaying warmth in return; and be glad to have us around. That point of happy, mutual acceptance is both the hinge upon which turns the other part of the paradox, and the clue to its resolution.

The second half of the paradox should be obvious. We have a commission to fulfil: a gospel of love to proclaim to a world which needs our message desperately. Christians should display all the enthusiasm, commitment, and fervour of the Jehovah's Witness I described, earlier. We should be as eager as him to see lives changed, and hearts, minds and souls won. The crucial question is: 'How do we set about our task?'

I believe that a humble, lively, loving Christian presence in the world, slow to judge, quick to serve, listening, and laughing, and accepting, is the most effective way of both witnessing to, and mediating, the Divine Love among God's children, in God's world. It isn't merely – or even primarily – a matter of talking. Often, that's the easy bit. Much more is required of us. If our lives belie the words we speak, if gloominess, or censoriousness, or exclusiveness, or hardness of heart cloak the joy and freedom and love we are supposed to have received, our witness becomes hollow, and is dismissed as a sham. We might fool the people in church, but across the gap we are soon rumbled, and a harsh verdict is passed. When that happens, we have not served our Lord very effectively.

If our glimpse of The Mystery and our understanding of the gospel have put love in our hearts, we will *love* people; and when people sense our love, they, too, will become more loving. If there is not love in our hearts, there is a danger that we shall make people more fit for hell than they were before they met us. I have known people I liked *more* before they became religious. It is perfectly possible to turn ordinary men and women into narrow-minded, world-denying, highly critical, glibly self-satisfied, fully assured, pompously 'saved', impertinent religious bigots. Jesus accused the Pharisees of doing that kind of thing, and we haven't lost the ability.

Mystery and gospel – the transcendent and the immanent, the unimaginable and the immediate, the holy and the tender – these are the interwoven, twin elements in the message we are trying to share. Crossing the gap with only one part of the message is not sufficient. On the one hand we say: 'Existence is tantalising; the universe – and all it contains, including our bodies – provokes awe and reverence. Don't lose your ability to wonder.' On the other hand we say: 'Jesus has given a vital clue to the meaning of human existence in His radical gospel of Love – the love we were designed to reflect but which, somehow, we seem to have forgotten. In the light of His emphasis on the centrality of love, *discover* yourselves, *become* yourselves, and *work* that the world might become *itself*: a place of beauty and inspiration and challenge; a place of justice and peace.'

Stripped of all the frills, that is our message to those who live on the other side of the gap, who seldom think in 'religious' terms or use 'religious' language. As we strive to proclaim it, and to practise what we preach, it is vital that we ask ourselves what it is that we are trying to achieve.

Our objectives are both personal and social. Like Jesus, we want to see a world which is brighter because a new dimension has been injected into human relationships. We are trying, I believe, to achieve three things.

First, we are trying to leaven and sweeten the quality of life in God's world: to increase the options and opportunities for growth and development – physical, mental, emotional, spiritual – *for all God's children*. Increasing the input of love will have this effect. A smile, a test ban treaty, a prayer, a bag of wheat, a touch, an errand, a housing programme, a shoulder to cry on, a book, a record, an apology, a visit, some medicine – positive things like these are all expressions of love, and as such contribute to raising the level of awareness and the quality of life in God's world. If they are not all direct acts of evangelism, they are not far removed.

Second, we are trying to encourage people to pause amid the clamour of our modern world and look searchingly at themselves – at their motives and attitudes – to see if the Divine Love is reflected there. We want people to recognise and explore the 'spiritual' dimension of life. I am not referring now to music, art and literature. They are some of the indispensable tools for the job (though they can easily become ends in themselves). I am referring to the great moral and spiritual dimension which embraces values, judgements, choices, personal priorities, standards of integrity and responsibility, conscience, good and evil, awe and wonder, beauty, truth and religion. We want people to seek, and to experience for themselves, the mystic realities of the inner life, which are as freely open to the shorthand-typist as to the bishop. These include the mystery and the joy of conversion, prayer, devotion and worship. *We are trying to point people to Christ.*

'It's taken you a long time to say that,' some will remark – and I agree. These first two evangelistic aims can be pursued a considerable distance without needing to set the significance of Christ in a narrow religious context. For that we should be grateful, and prepared to act accordingly. A simple 'Come to Jesus' approach has only a minimal appeal beyond the gap. It carries little meaning, and gains only an occasional, isolated response. But setting our message in a broader context achieves far more. It makes the world a brighter place and gets people thinking. The right to press the claims of Jesus has to be worked for and won, my side of the gap. Short cuts can easily have the effect of making the gap wider.

Third, we are trying to win members for the church. Of course we are! While I have placed it at the bottom of my list, and although it is, in one sense, entirely different from the first two objectives, this aim is vitally important. If the church is the focus and symbol of Christ's continuing presence in the world, the guardian of His message of Love, and itself a loving, accepting, healing community, we need new members continually, to ensure that the message is shared with each generation. Today, the need has become pressing.

We have no cause to feel ashamed of what we are offering, and no reason to be embarrassed for seeking new members. Divine worship, Christian fellowship, and the study and practice of religion in its myriad forms are potentially stimulating, enriching, and fulfilling experiences in themselves. We are *not* just trying to fill pews; we are offering something good!

Public worship itself constitutes an important form of evangelism, especially the pastoral occasions – christenings, weddings, and funerals. This particular evangelistic opportunity falls mainly to the clergy, and is the subject of a later chapter. One matter, however, must be mentioned at this point. I hear of churches where certain pastoral offices are frequently withheld from applicants on the grounds of their lack of active Christian commitment and non-attendance at worship. Infants are denied baptism, and weddings are refused. I recognise a certain logic in this approach, but I cannot share it. On the contrary, I have to say, plainly, that such an attitude is, to me, not only unacceptable, tactically inept and theologically disastrous; it is offensive. By now, you should be able to guess why!

God loves us all: not just those with religious inclinations; not just the people who cry 'Lord, Lord', but every man, woman and child. And God rejoices in any spark of idealism, any fleeting awareness of that other dimension, any tentative response to The Mystery. When primitive man acknowledged his smallness and worshipped the objects which overawed or frightened him – like certain trees, or the sun, or thunder – God understood. When primitive man sought the help of the gods in attempts to ensure fertility, good harvests, and victory in battle, God understood. When, today, men and women estranged from organised religion still experience the need for rite and ritual to express their sense of wonder when confronted by the mysteries of birth, love, and death, God still understands. So should we. It is not for us to quench the smoking flax, but to use our expertise to raise it to a flame.

Incidentally, I would not dare to refuse infant baptism. 'Suffer the little children to come unto me, and forbid them not' could not be more explicit. Infant baptism is between God and the child. Priest, parents, godparents and church members play minor roles. It is one of the purest proclamations of the gospel, signifying that God's love for us exists before we are aware of it, exists before we sin, is unbroken by our sin, and endures for ever. (I shall emphasise those words again, later.) All pastoral occasions are, for the minister, supreme evangelistic opportunities, not to 'push' religion on a captive audience dressed up for the occasion, but by his or her bearing and accepting attitude, by his conduct of the worship, and by his combination of reverence with warmth and humanity, to communicate the Divine Love. 'Him that cometh to me I will in no wise cast out.'

Evangelism takes various forms, and over the years many brave attempts have been made to present the gospel effectively in our ever-changing contemporary society. Some types of evangelism seem to have more bite than others, but the test question is simply: 'Will it work?' If there is a chance that any venture in outreach may touch even a few people not normally reached by the work of the church, it's worth a try.

The obligation to evangelise is the responsibility of the entire church, but within that context, the New Testament asserts that among the different ministries to which God calls – and for which He equips – men and women, some are called to be evangelists. I believe many more are called than hear, recognise, and respond to their spiritual vocation. Perhaps God is calling *you*?

For those who wish to contribute to the missionary work of the modern church here in Britain, I have some practical advice. If you have caught a vision of Jesus, and long to share it – long to share *Him* – this is one of the first things you should do. Look at your community, or your neighbourhood. Each locality has what I term 'focal points' – centres of influence, or meeting-places. Draw up a list. Consider it carefully. Select one venue. *Then leap across the gap.* Get in – and stay in! Establish a link. Don't spell it out why you are there! Don't hand out leaflets! Don't recite a digest of last Sunday morning's sermon to the first person kind enough to speak to you! 'Just hold your noise,' as my mother used to tell me. Simply try to be yourself; a face in the crowd. If, at first, you feel new and slightly awkward, unsure of the 'rules' and ill at ease, you have discovered how your new companions feel when they cross the gap in the opposite direction and enter a church. Play for time. Increasingly, you will become recognised and welcomed. Be patient. Think of yourself as one of God's secret agents. Enjoy yourself. But never forget your commission.

When I became a bus driver, I kept a low profile for as long as possible. I told a few people I was a minister, but I didn't make a big thing of it. I wanted to be treated like any other newcomer. If everyone had known that I sometimes wore a dog-collar, it would have affected their attitude to me. Some would have been extra polite; others, uncomfortable, would have been extra rude. Both would have been false reactions. I waited many, many months, learning and watching. In the meantime, I was authorised to minister in a local parish church where I had established an ecumenical team ministry with an Anglican colleague.

In God's own time my 'unveiling' came – and it happened in a manner I could never have imagined or engineered in a thousand years. I went, one evening, to my trade union branch meeting. The small upstairs room was filled to overflowing. A contentious issue had arisen since the meeting had been arranged, and now every member of the branch wanted to be present. With angry busmen packing the stairs and spilling over into the street, the committee was in a fix. Suddenly, I knew that the moment for which I had been waiting had arrived. Not daring to wait, in case my courage failed, I stood up, held high the keys of the parish church, told the chairman it was empty and at the disposal of the branch – and flopped down! The committee members were hardly aware of my existence, but they were in no position to look a gift horse in the mouth. With alacrity, relief and genuine gratitude, the meeting was adjourned to the church. I had forgotten it was bell-ringers' practice night, but it seemed appropriate that the bells should be ringing out as the old church filled with drivers and conductors. As I looked round the beautiful and familiar building packed with my new friends and workmates, the two parts of my life moved into conjunction, and I was deeply touched.

The events of that evening made the national dailies, and passed into the folk-lore of the bus garage. But, to me, their importance was even greater. My secret was out! Some liked me, some probably didn't – but at least I had been judged as a person, not as a parson. Proof that I had been right to adopt an almost over-cautious waiting game came from the several busmen who, despite the many hours already spent together at work and in the canteen, found it difficult – for several weeks – to treat me in their normal, relaxed manner. But from that day onward, a trickle of canteen discussions and pastoral requests and opportunities began, which swelled eventually to a flood.

So, when you cross the gap – wait! And *eventually*, opportunities will come for you to reveal – undramatically and casually – your first and greatest Love. Those moments may come quickly, or you may have to wait a very long time before the wonderful opportunity arises naturally to name the Name and to commend your Lord. It will be such a lovely and alarming moment it will make all the waiting seem worthwhile.

But don't undervalue the waiting. All the while – if your spiritual life is maintained, if you are nourished by Word and Sacrament – you will be gently radiating the Divine Love. On strange and alien territory, it all may seem too nerve-racking at first: but if you stick to it, refuse to turn back or throw in your hand, you will eventually and inevitably become an integral part of that scene. You will secure a bridge-head and a foothold; and God will have a representative, eager to co-operate and do His will, in a part of His world He knows and loves and inhabits, but where – on the other side of the gap – He is often unloved and unacknowledged.

There are many 'focal points' in every district. A few of us are better equipped to penetrate some of them than others, and no one can enter them all. But there is a place, near you, which *you* could enter, for God. Public houses, social clubs, youth centres, gardening clubs, political centres, protest movements – wherever people assemble in such a manner that an impact is made on the community, *we should aim to have somebody present*. This is a policy of deliberate infiltration, like the communists used for years. It stands in stark contrast to the pattern of withdrawal from the world into which many Christians (if not entire denominations) have been known to slip. It is what we celebrate each Christmas.

If I thought that large doses of the old-fashioned, direct evangelistic approach still worked – the open-air meetings, the door-to-door visits (both of which, perhaps, may still have a place) – I would throw myself into them whole-heartedly. I suspect, however, that, by and large, they are the tools of another age. But the approach I am recommending to those called to be evangelists will never be out of date because – like Christianity itself – it represents a principle to be applied, not a detailed programme. *You* have to fill in the details!

Be imaginative when you draw up your list. Remember

that Saturday lunch-time in your local feels different from Friday night; perhaps you could tackle one, but not the other. If you live in a rural area, don't forget the village football team. The players and supporters form a group which meets together regularly throughout the winter. Involvement and interest in the club could lead to many valuable new contacts. Remember, too, that some gatherings are totally unstructured, yet very important. I am thinking, now, of the crowd of youths who used to congregate every night of the week on the same corner of a High Street in a large village, with their motorbikes and girlfriends – and, for all I know, may do so still. A Christian youngster who was part of that scene would be doing vital work for God. My best evangelistic opportunities – God forgive me for not making more of them – have arisen from bus garage and public house contacts. But it's no use crossing the gap and 'getting in' for a fortnight. We need to get in – and stay till closing-time!

To be a disciple of Jesus, you don't have to be 'important' or 'special'. Your very weakness and vulnerability may prove to be your greatest strength. I served my shrievalty under a Lord Mayor who was confined to a wheelchair. To some, we seemed an unpromising pair, and they looked askance when our term of office began. 'One in a wheelchair, the other a parson . . .' Neither of us had anything to lose! But David Bradford was a practising Christian, a man of humility and humanity, compassion and laughter: and Thelma, his wife, made an outstanding Lady Mayoress – homely, intelligent and sincere. Molly and I enjoyed every moment we shared with them in the service of the city. By the time our year had ended, we had more than achieved our ambition. We had assumed the ancient offices, polished and brightened them, and handed them on to our successors in good condition. In between, we had represented the city in our own distinctive way. To our surprise, we were not only recognised constantly in the streets; we were

accorded a measure of acceptance and affection overwhelming in its warmth and breadth.

Commitment, courage and a consecrated imagination:
these must be the marks of a twentieth-century evangelist if
we are to penetrate effectively beyond the gap. Even if it
means shedding some of our church duties, more of us must
get out among the people who have stopped coming to us.
We have to provide a deliberate Christian presence in the
community. Our absenteeism is our greatest sin. *Being there*
is what counts. Being there, not necessarily because you
want to be there, but for God. Being there, in good times
and in bad. Being there, as points of acceptance, and
warmth, and love. Being there, waiting patiently, praying
silently, alert and positive, serving the days of your apprenticeship, and earning the right to speak. Being there, ready
for the encounter in which your Lord will come.

Don't worry about finding the right words to say. When
the time comes to speak, the words will be given. Don't
worry if – within the church – you provoke mild criticism
or even outright disapproval. ('We don't see so much of
you, these days . . .'; 'Whatever is he thinking about,
spending all his time in a place like that? . . .') Nothing
changes; they said the same things about Jesus: 'This man
receiveth sinners, and eateth with them.' At least you
won't go to hell with clean hands. My apprenticeship was
served long ago, so my witness is forthright and bois-
terous; but I still don't 'push' religion . . .

No reproach will deflect the evangelist who has consciously
taken his cue from his Lord. In the fullness of time, and
moved by the Divine Love, Christ plunged from the heart of
the Godhead into the icy turbulence of this crazy, sin-torn,
wonderful world, with all its suffering and with all its tenderness. He doesn't want us, or anybody else, to be plucked out
of it. He wants us to love it. And to love one another.

4

Thy Kingdom Come

I begin with some verses to set the scene. First, Tennyson and the psalmist on the brevity of this mysterious existence we share:

> The woods decay, the woods decay and fall,
> The vapours weep their burthen to the ground,
> Man comes and tills the field and lies beneath,
> And after many a summer dies the swan.

> The days of our years are threescore years and ten,
> or even by reason of strength fourscore years;
> yet is their pride but labour and sorrow;
> for it is soon gone, and we fly away.

The psalmist, again, on the illusion of ownership and the centrality of stewardship:

> The earth is the Lord's,
> and all that therein is . . .

Finally, Jesus of Nazareth on the politically devastating simplicity of the family principle which lies at the heart of his teaching:

> Our Father . . .

Christians have always fought on behalf of the poor, the underprivileged, the sick, and the exploited; *but too many Christians have avoided the fight*. They have given – often with great generosity – to worthy causes and to people in need; but they have steered clear of radical political involvement; which is a pity, for political action is the way the world gets changed. Anything else is first aid.

Despite the traditions exemplified by people like F.D. Maurice, Charles Kingsley, Hugh Price Hughes, William

Temple and Donald Soper; despite many bold and authoritative statements on social issues; despite the courageous witness of groups and individuals, there remains a great gap between the church and those who are engaged in political activity and are working for the creation of a just society.

At one level, I can sympathise. There is more than one way of contributing to the well-being of the community; and there are only a certain number of hours in the week; and nobody can do everything. Political, economic, and social concerns are invariably complicated, and many of us find it difficult to understand the issues, let alone make reasoned and responsible judgements. Jesus lived a long time ago; the structure of modern society is incomparably more complex than that which governed the ancient world in the days of Jesus and the prophets and the apostles. All these reflections are true. None provides a legitimate excuse for ignoring the social, corporate, political dimension of the gospel message of Love.

Nevertheless, a great number of sincere churchgoers appear unmindful of the social implications inherent in Christian discipleship. There are, conversely, many splendid men and women of idealism and costly social commitment, active in political party and council chamber, whose *private* lives, however, are less commendable. Bitchiness, backbiting, and other unattractive features contrast glaringly with the brightness of their social endeavours. Both groups are displaying aspects of the Divine Love: the first, primarily, in personal relationships and attitudes; the second in service to the community and in political involvement. But neither is displaying the full, rounded, wholeness of the Love which is the hallmark of those whose first allegiance is to the Kingdom of God – that invisible, spiritual realm whose currency is tenderness, compassion, forbearance, justice, and peace.

Love is indivisible. In all who claim to take seriously the life of Christ, the same caring attitude of openness and warmth should characterise not only their pesonal relationships, but also their approach to social and political issues – local, national, and international.

Christian discipleship is founded upon, and is an expression of, the wonder of the Holy Trinity. This cannot be emphasised too often, nor too strongly. Unbalanced and incomplete expressions of the Christian religion usually indicate a defective trinitarian theology. Discipleship embraces the awe and reverence provoked by The Mystery – by the universe, the people in it, and our own existence. It embraces the humanity, the tenderness, and the self-sacrificial service inspired by Jesus. It embraces the re-born will and the new joy and strength which we believe it is possible for men and women to experience, and which we attribute to the Holy Spirit, the Eternal Activist, the Eternal Lover. The Christian, therefore, is committed to a way of life which is 'other-worldly', *very* worldly, and which has access to power. This truth should be remembered constantly when the gap between the church and those actively committed to the pursuit of social justice is examined.

Above all, Christian discipleship is an experience of liberation. In renouncing the selfishness into which we have fallen (and putting ourselves on guard against it); and in committing ourselves to the Way of Love demonstrated by Jesus (in His life, death, and resurrection; in the stories of the miracles, and the parables of the Kingdom), *we are set free*. This is not clerical rhetoric. We are liberated in a remarkably profound and definite sense. Christ's revelation of a universe powered by Love means that, in responding, we are coming home; we are truly discovering *ourselves*; we are being released from the vicious circles of hate-begetting hatred and love-destroying selfishness.

Once we have accepted Christ's Way as our personal philosophy, and stepped into the Kingdom of Love, our freedom can never again be taken from us. It is this which has so infuriated the persecutors of Christians, from Roman times to the days of Hitler, and into our own age. We can be mocked, imprisoned or discriminated against; we can be destroyed; but that commitment to the Way of Love, which includes the forgiveness of our enemies, cannot be taken from us. We may be poor, or denied justice, or suffer all manner of deprivation against which we have every right to protest; but the liberty of the spirit – and it is a *real* liberty, which many who are rich and powerful do not possess – while plainly linked to our physical circumstances, is ultimately utterly distinct from them. 'Stone walls do not a prison make . . .' Drugs, or extreme cruelty, may distort personality, and may extract from me confessions and recantations: but those are meaningless, and worthless to lovers of Truth, if obtained by my abuse.

Those who say 'Yes' to Love enter a new dimension: a new way of living and thinking. I am anxious to add my personal testimony (though words sound feeble and inadequate). Long ago, through the preaching of the gospel, Jesus gave me a 'vision' of a *world* of love. He gave me a glimpse of *myself* as, potentially, a loving person. In the moment when I wanted both those pictures to come true, He invited me into His Kingdom and set me free, and at large. It happened to Nicodemus, who came to Jesus by night. It happened to the woman by the well in Samaria – of whom more later – when Jesus offered her Living Water. It happens in all kinds of ways, and marks the point at which true discipleship begins. Already, the momentous social implications of such an experience should be obvious.

Yet, looking in from outside, I have to say, with a heavy heart, that the social witness of many Christians does not appear very convincing. It lacks the authentic notes which command attention, and challenge and convict. Our life-styles cause people to wonder how seriously we take our religion. Perhaps we should pause, more frequently, to remind ourselves what it means to follow Jesus.

We are committed to walking through each day in an attitude of love. Our example, our inspiration, and our source of strength is the life of Jesus. The ancient religion in which he was brought up knew nothing of rigid distinctions between personal holiness and social righteousness. Isaiah put it in a nutshell:

> The kind of fasting I want is this: Remove the chains of oppression and the yoke of injustice, and let the oppressed go free. Share your food with the hungry and open your homes to the homeless poor. Give clothes to those who have nothing to wear . . . Then my favour will shine on you like the morning sun.

Amos was fierce in his denunciations of those who exploited the poor:

> O ye that swallow up the needy . . . falsifying the balances by deceit [attaching weights to the under-side of the scales] . . . buy the poor for silver and the needy for a pair of shoes . . .

But, above all, the prophets had a goal at which to aim. They looked forward, with strong confidence, to a new age of peace and justice which, one day, would dawn when 'The wolf shall dwell with the lamb . . and a little child shall lead them'; when 'they shall beat their swords into ploughshares, and their spears into pruninghooks'; when 'nation shall not lift up sword against nation, neither shall they learn war any more'; when 'instead of the thorn shall come up the fir tree, and instead of the brier shall come up the myrtle tree'; when 'they shall obtain joy and gladness, and sorrow and sighing shall flee away'.

The longing for social justice; the fearless condemnation of social evils; the vision of a new society – many of the most stirring faces of Love are present in the Old Testament, and these were all part of the religious heritage of Jesus. For his part, he lived a life devoid of privilege and status. He was born in the stable of an inn, of an unmarried peasant girl. He worked as a labouring man, a carpenter. Later, he had no home to call his own, remarking wryly that – compared with him – the foxes and birds were well off!

He opened his ministry by quoting Isaiah:

The spirit of the Lord is upon me. He has sent me to announce good news to the poor . . . to proclaim release for prisoners, and recovery of sight for the blind.

In the Sermon on the Mount, he described the Way of Love and made plain who take precedence in the Kingdom: the poor in spirit; they that mourn; they that hunger and thirst after righteousness: the merciful; the pure in heart; the peacemakers; they that are persecuted for righteousness' sake. Later, to the question: 'Lord, when saw we thee an hungred, or athirst, or a stranger, or naked, or sick, or in prison, and did not minister unto thee?' he replied: 'Inasmuch as ye did it not to one of the least of these my brethren, ye did it not to me'.

He warned, bluntly, that it was easier for a camel to pass through the eye of a needle than for a rich man to enter the Kingdom. He told the parable of the Good Samaritan, ending with those five stunning, staccato words: 'Go, and do thou likewise.' Finally, he was executed as a common criminal, not for his devotional practices, not for his teaching on prayer, or his love of the Psalms, but because he constituted a political threat.

After his death, his followers strove to understand and express the meaning of his life and passion and resurrection: 'They had all things common, and sold their possessions and goods, and parted them to all men, as every man had need.'

Not many of those first Christians were wise or rich or noble, by conventional standards. St Paul admitted: 'God hath chosen the foolish things of the world to confound the wise . . . and the weak things of the world to confound the things which are mighty.'

St John, who once, perhaps, leaned on Jesus' breast at the Last Supper, said:

> If a man has enough to live on, and yet when he sees his brother in need shuts up his heart against him, how can it be said that the divine love dwells in him? My children, love must not be a matter of words or talk; it must be genuine, and show itself in action.

Much more, in a similar vein, can be found in the epistle of St James:

> If ye fulfil the royal law according to the scripture, 'Thou shalt love thy neighbour as thyself', ye do well . . .

> But ye have despised the poor . . .

> Ye have respect to him that weareth the gay clothing, and say unto him, 'Sit thou here in a good place'; and say to the poor, 'Stand thou there . . .'

> If a brother or sister be naked, and destitute of daily food, and one of you say unto them, 'Depart in peace, be ye warmed and filled'; notwithstanding ye give them not those things which are needful to the body; what doth it profit? . . . Even so faith, if it hath not works, is dead . .

Finally, at the Bible's end, amid the strange, apocalyptic scenes depicted in the Revelation of St John the Divine, are inspiring lines which seem to summarise all that has gone before:

And I saw a new heaven and a new earth . . .

And the leaves of the tree were for the healing of the nations . . .

That selection of references is made on a purely personal basis, but I believe it represents faithfully – rather than distorts – the biblical position on four important matters.

First, it demonstrates the truth that personal religion cannot be separated from social and political attitudes. In Joe Orton's film script, *Up Against It*, one of the main characters, Christopher Low, makes the plea:

I'm hungry and thirsty. I need help.

To which Mrs O'Scullan replies, crisply:

I'm not interested in your private life.

Such an attitude is diametrically opposed to the insights of the gospel. There, hunger and thirst and a cry for help are not private problems but social priorities demanding the attention of us all. To the Christian, justice is simply the Love of which Jesus spoke, expressed in social terms.

Second, it highlights the paradox that, while God is our ultimate destiny, eternity is a mystery; for the moment, there is work to be done here and now which has eternal significance. Upon our treatment of each other hang great issues.

Third, it reveals the fact that throughout the Bible, the poor, the deprived, the vulnerable and the disadvantaged are portrayed as possessing a special place in the affections of Almighty God.

Fourth, it suggests that in situations of complexity, which present a variety of choices and approaches, Christians should opt to support and stand alongside the less privileged – even when, technically, they may be in the wrong. And where risks have to be taken in this unjust and imperfect world, Christians should generally throw in their lot on the side of peace, justice, and radical social change – even at the risk, sometimes, of looking foolish. How wide yawns the gap, at this point! How often, from positions of immaculate respectability, church members leave it to people who profess no religion to stand up for Love and humanity!

During the miners' strike a few years ago, the labour movement in my locality 'adopted' the families of the striking miners of a Nottinghamshire pit. Each week, large sums of money were raised, and every Sunday a convoy of vehicles carried food and other necessities 120 miles to help stock the soup kitchen which had opened there. This venture did not last for just a few weeks. It continued for months. An open-ended pledge was given: 'We will stand by you thoughout this terrible experience, for as long as it continues . . .' This became one of the most impressive examples of sustained, practical, costly solidarity – love in action – I have ever witnessed.

The miners' strike was a messy, violent and controversial dispute, but this operation was one in which all Christians should have been able to participate – if only on humanitarian grounds. While the rights and wrongs of the issue were being debated and bitter battles were being fought, *families were in need*. It's worth risking your 'reputation' in a situation like that. The temptation to tread cautiously for fear of being in some way compromised is unworthy. 'Safety first' is not a Christian slogan.

Christians are committed, above all else, to reflecting – in their actions and their attitudes – the Divine Love as they perceive it revealed in Jesus. I want that thought to run through these pages like the responses in a litany because it is the first principle of discipleship. It seems, however, not to be widely understood. The gap between the abundant life of Jesus and the quality of our Christian witness should alarm us; but many Christians don't even see the problem, and are blissfully unaware that occasional attendance at worship and generous donations to the church are not enough. Following Jesus means more than that.

The life we are offered in the Kingdom has a distinctive quality. For example, we should be able – like Jesus himself – to mix easily with the rich as well as the poor, behaving naturally, shunning jealousy, accepting kindness graciously – yet always taking care to preserve our integrity. If wealthy or influential people show generosity or friendship towards us, we should accept with gladness and humility: though they must be prepared for the consequences! They must understand that, on many issues, we will not agree with them; that we long to see society changed; that we would gladly see their riches taken from them and redistributed. But if, knowing these things, they smile at our foolishness and naivety, are confident we can never harm them, and still invite us to the party because they like us as human beings, we should not stay away. Any barriers between us, at a personal level, should never be of our raising.

Wherever we are, we should never appear proud or self-assertive, but humble, sitting at table – as Jesus instructed – in the lowest places, counting others more worthy than ourselves. We should display attitudes of acceptance and concern, respect and courtesy, warmth and humour, in all our relationships. We should never be afraid to stand alone, however powerful the opponents ranged against us – particularly to protest when injustice or suffering is inflicted upon others. This we must do even when it means criticising religious leaders, (and I shall give an example in a moment).

Because our glimpse of Jesus has liberated and set us free, we are concerned *only* to be channels of the Divine Love, seeking no reward, no status, no personal advancement: only the quiet joy and the inward peace given to those who are true to the Truth revealed in Christ. We do not court hardship, but we endure persecution with patience, try to make light of it, and attempt to return good for evil, rather than be disloyal to the Kingdom and betray the vision.

Meekness is a key virtue, crucial to faithful discipleship. It does not mean weakness, but the opposite: great strength, under perfect control. Children, the old, the sick, the dying, the quaint, and the poor all merit our patience, respect and friendship. They are senior to us, in the Kingdom. The defenceless, and those in need of any kind, should receive our attention and our affection, ungrudgingly. We should treat all whom we meet – whatever their condition – in the same open manner, taking each one seriously.

Christians are conscious of being engaged in a struggle against dark powers which create disharmony and discord; conscious, too, of the corrosive and corruptive effects of great wealth. Yet Christians love God's world and all its wonders. We are not opposed to material well-being; but because Jesus taught us to say 'Our Father', we recognise all men and women as our brothers and sisters. As *stewards* of the wealth and resources entrusted to us, we acknowledge that they were intended not for our personal benefit alone, but for the family; and we are anxious that everyone should enjoy their just and equitable portion, and live in peace and unity and harmony.

This is the life of the Kingdom. It has a serenity, a poise and a balance which transcends parties, boundaries, denominations and divisions. It has a tenderness which sees no shame in tears. It revels in the freedom which knows it can never be imprisoned without its own consent. It is confident and strong in the knowledge that 'underneath are the everlasting arms'. It is rooted and grounded in Love.

Suddenly, at the centre of Christian discipleship, we encounter, again, the wonder and The Mystery. The Divine Love is an Eternal Love. It exists in every place and in every age; within time and beyond time. This insight supplies the final dimension to our understanding of discipleship and the life of the Kingdom. It reminds us that we should live in the light of eternity, conscious of life's brevity, and mindful that 'we all do fade as a leaf'. Another paradox has emerged. We are wholly committed to God's world: committed to extending the Kingdom of love and righteousness. Yet there is a lightness to our touch as we move through the world. We do not grasp, or hoard, or cling tightly to things which needs must pass away. We are citizens, together, of planet Earth; but, in St Paul's phrase, we are also 'citizens of heaven'. Our firmest hold should be upon things unseen.

We remember, too, that the church speaks of judgement, and of accounting, some day, for our stewardship: 'Son, remember that thou in thy lifetime receivedst thy good things . . .' Life is so brief! Whatever our destiny, let's walk tall, and do right while we *are* here. That is the note which an awareness of eternity injects into Christian living. We are both committed and detached. The Kingdom is at hand: Love is waiting to break into our lives the moment we say 'Yes' to Love. The Kingdom is within us: when Love reigns there. We seek the Kingdom: when we work towards a social order which is in harmony with the principle of the Divine Love, and within which men and women will display compassion and righteousness. For this we pray: Thy Kingdom come! And yet: the Kingdom is not of this world.

If my description of Christian discipleship is accurate only in part, it is obvious that we face many serious problems of credibility, all of which are expressions of 'the gap'. Five disturbing factors leap immediately to mind.

First, many Christians give every appearance of being very comfortably off. They must answer, of course, for themselves. There is no clear incomes policy laid down in the New Testament! The world is good and matter is good – that is why we want everyone to be able to enjoy creation to the utmost, and to realise their full potential. But it is hard to reconcile the possesion of great personal wealth, in a world of want and deprivation, with the teaching and the example of a homeless carpenter. We go to great lengths to square the circle, but it cannot easily be done. On the contrary, all too often our bank account denies us the right to speak.

Second, some Christians are incredibly insensitive in the thoughtless manner they parade their wealth. It is one thing for people to reconcile themselves to not being able to afford luxuries which have become commonplace among other sections of the community. It is rubbing it in when they have to hear about, or keep admiring, somebody else's new car or exotic foreign holiday. However, such trivial incidents pale to insigificance compared with the way we must seem to vaunt our wealth before the starving millions. Whatever do our needy brethren make of us? And then we wonder why we can't see Jesus very clearly . . .

Third, too few Christians are politically active. If this is understandable in part, it is nonetheless regrettable. Those who believe in God the Creator, and in Jesus the Incarnate Son, should try to make a contribution, however small, where it matters.

Fourth, some Christians profess political neutrality. Apart from being a typical piece of cowardly ecclesiastical buck-passing, this claim is a naive illusion, a sham and a lie. It is impossible to avoid adopting a political stance, because we are all members of the community. We adopt either a positive stance or a negative one – but the negative is just as political as the positive. I certainly don't believe the church should take out corporate membership of any particular political party. The church is not that kind of organisation. But if we say the church should not be involved in politics, and we leave the political arguments to those who like that sort of thing (in the way that we happen to like religion), politically we are supporting the status quo – which, far from being neutral, is an attitude with immense political implications. It also leaves us completely cut off from all who *are* involved in political activity and working to create a better world. It is not enough to hope, vaguely, that some things may change in the future – then add, in effect: 'But for the moment, well, we'll carry on . . .' Is that *really* a tenable position for members of a movement which, in its earliest days, was accused of turning the world upside down? Leaving it to people who do not pretend to be religious to stand up and speak out on behalf of those God cares about most, is not only despicable. It shatters credibility, and makes the gap permanent.

Fifth, Christians look, too often, for a middle way. Coming from someone who endeavours to cultivate a balanced, rounded, catholic spirit, that may sound surprising! There is, however, a type of moderation which is not a faithful interpretation of the gospel. Some political parties are historically associated with – and continue to receive support from, represent, and work in the interests of – the powerful and the privileged. Others, traditionally, side with the less privileged and the underprivileged. Some Christians, for various reasons, are inclined to split the difference. The decision, of course, is theirs. Sometimes the middle way *is* the best way: but not always, nor automatically. 'Moderation' can have an insidious appeal to Christians. The word can be used as an excuse to avoid decisive and painful action. It is seldom a virtue in the face of great evil. The reason why those who belong to the Kingdom should risk commitment to policies aimed at creating fundamental changes in an unjust world is that, for millions, things could hardly be worse.

Our political attitudes and our social witness should spring from secure spiritual foundations – from a recognition, and an acceptance in our hearts, of the basic, fundamental principle of Love. It isn't enough simply to pray or to hope. We have to pass from theory to practice: our insights and principles have to be translated into parties and policies and action and votes. Political parties, like churches, are imperfect institutions. I support the party which approximates most closely to my ideal.

I would like to see a political party take seriously the family principle of the gospel, and the revolutionary principle of the Kingdom that 'the first shall be last and the last first'. I would like it to make the priority of the poor the central plank of its manifesto and say to the nation: '*Whatever* resources are available, we will first of all provide imaginatively and generously for the elderly, the sick, the housebound, the blind, deaf, the dumb, the children, the physically and mentally handicapped, the deprived, the lonely, and the weak. When *they* have been cared for, then we will look at other matters; but nothing will take priority over those who are vulnerable. A family may tighten its belt if times are hard, but it never makes its weakest members bear the brunt.' Such an intention, clearly stated, would strike a chord in many hearts. People would *know* that it was right. 'Seek ye first the kingdom of God, and his righteousness; and all these things shall be added unto you.'

Gospel insights should help us to face even painful and complex issues bravely and positively. Unemployment provides one example. God, in His creation, has supplied the raw materials we need for our requirements. To turn them into the goods we desire, we have to work, in harmony both with the creation and with each other. We don't all work at the same tasks. We work as a team. We co-operate, and share, and exchange our skills and our products. We need one another.

Work can be boring, repetitive, grinding and soul-destroying, as well as creative and fulfilling. If advances in technology mean there is less drudgery, so much the better. But idleness, and a sense of uselessness, and the feeling of not being able to contribute to the common wealth are evil, and never more so than when young people, on the threshold of life, are the victims. We are bad managers, that is part of our trouble; and we forget we are members of a family.

The work which remains should be shared as evenly and sensibly as possible. Those for whom there is no prospect of paid employment should be provided for generously and justly, receiving their necessities and allowances not as grudging hand-outs, but as of right: as part of the family. Then unemployment need not be the end of experience, the end of dignity and self-respect, the scrap-heap, or the end of life. In a society which had caught a vision of the Kingdom of God, so-called unemployment could become a creative experience. Being unemployed should not mean we can no longer contribute to the community. Nobody can be blamed if suitable paid work is not available – *but a contribution to the life of the community can be made in many ways*. If I were unfortunate enough to be unemployed, I like to think that it might be possible to spend a certain number of days working voluntarily, perhaps with the handicapped. I would hope to have two days a week in the countryside – that is, enjoying the swiftly-passing, precious gift of life in the way I enjoy most. The remainder of my time would be devoted to religious and political activities aimed at extending the Kingdom of God and increasing the opportunities for the maximum number of people to live as fully as possible, in the ways *they* most enjoy.

It will be obvious to all that I write as a busman and a man of religion rather than as a politician! My dream of a manifesto and my thoughts on unemployment and wealth are childish in their simplicity. They do not pretend to begin to constitute a political programme. Yet I hope they reflect attitudes which have their origin in the biblical themes of the Kingdom of God, the Fatherhood of God, and the brotherhood and sisterhood of men and women. Our common life should be about caring and sharing – about *loving*; that's the basic New Testament principle. It forms the backbone and skeleton of all Christian social thought and action. The political flesh we add to the skeleton depends upon a variety of factors including our temperament, the quality of our commitment, the democratic institutions and instruments of change available to us, and our perception of the political realities.

When I am able to attend political gatherings, the number of fellow-churchmen I meet is small and disappointing. (Perhaps I go to the wrong places!) 'Am I my brother's keeper?' Cain's indignant question has been repeated many times. The answer, of course, is 'No! You are your brother's brother.' We must love our brothers and sisters; and go to their aid. I cannot help wishing that Christ's followers were better known for the simplicity of their lives, in an age when resources are being squandered and millions starve. Alas, we appear as acquisitive as the rest. We needn't go about with long faces; we shouldn't begrudge a treat, or a party, or a meal with friends. Jesus rebuked the cold, petty, 'practical', legalistic attitude of Judas on this very issue, when Mary took the ointment of spikenard, 'very costly', and anointed the feet of Jesus because she loved him. Judas protested that it would better have been sold on behalf of the poor. How sincere he was we cannot tell; certainly, he wasn't very imaginative. We *need* little moments of celebration, or luxury, or relaxation, to recharge the batteries and prepare ourselves to continue the battle. But we don't need enormous bank balances. Jesus didn't have them. Money can be used to achieve great good; but if we cling to it tightly, it becomes a burden. 'If riches increase, set not your heart upon them.' When Jesus sets us free, the love of money is one of the chains from which we are released. The freedom he gives is not a licence to do whatever we please, regardless of the consequences. It is, rather, the freedom of Love, and enables us to work – without fear or favour or ulterior motive – for justice and for peace.

Many immense social issues confront our generation, and if our vison of Jesus was clearer – if our hearts were liberated and filled with Love – we would be more to the fore in helping to tackle them. I want to refer, briefly, to three, selected (almost at random) for their importance and because *too many* Christians are separated from the heat of the battle, and are leaving the fight to others. 'Not every one that saith unto me, Lord, Lord . . . but he that doeth the will . . .'

I was shamed into rejoining the Campaign for Nuclear Disarmament – after a long, lethargic lapse – by the witness of a number of young busmen at the garage. They had no time for church, yet seemed to be speaking the language of the Kingdom with authority, while I was lamely hedging my bets, and looking pathetic. I believe that the survival of the planet is more important than 'defence', and risks have to be taken, gestures made, to break the vicious circles of fear which have long threatened to engulf us in nuclear night. Sometimes we are called to speak prophetically, not as Christians, nor as Britons, but as human beings to the human race.

From the question of nuclear power, it is only a short step to a host of environmental issues. Every Christian, *as an integral part of discipleship*, should actively support at least one conservation movement. The depletion of the ozone layer, the destruction of the rain-forests, the pollution of oceans and rivers, the production of acid rain, the destruction of hedgerows, the activities of whalers and big-game hunters – all these, when added to the chilling risks associated with nuclear power, combine to cast a cloud of uncertainty over the future of life on Earth.

'Even if the bomb drops, I know where I'll go,' an evangelical Christian, who had no time for political involvement, once said to me. Such sentiments are usually an affront to the Christian doctrines of Creation and Incarnation. Knowledge and faith of that order should in fact, provide a spur to disinterested political service in the name of humanity, and in the name of all the other creatures to whom, also, this planet is home. *The world matters to God.* He made it, He loves it, He upholds it, He visited it. The ox and ass in the Christmas story have enormous symbolic significance, reminding us that the whole Creation was involved when Love came down. The message of Love has not only human but cosmic implications; and because we have not learned and accepted the message, the planet could die.

'Love was His meaning' said Mother Julian (who lived half a mile up the street from where I am writing these words). Love for each other, in personal relationships – which means friendship and kindness; love for each other, in social relationships – which means justice and peace; and love for the Creation – which means reverence and responsible stewardship. The message of Jesus, therefore, has a direct bearing on what we have come to call green issues.

But it takes, perhaps, an issue like gay rights to wrong-foot the followers of Jesus most completely, and leave them stranded on one side of a gap, in strange and unlovely company, while the kindest and most sensible members of the community gaze across, in sadness and amazement, from the other. The hatred, fear and suspicion to which homosexuals are still frequently subjected, and the various forms of persecution and ridicule they have to endure, are totally alien to the spirit of Christ. The ignorance which refuses to understand that human sexuality is a spectrum containing no clear division between heterosexuals and homosexuals, and cannot grasp that to be gay in orientation is as morally neutral as ginger hair, blue eyes and left-handedness, is to be deplored when so much knowledge is now available.

One Sunday I walked out of a service when I felt that hatred of gays was being preached. Later, as I reflected, I couldn't help suspecting that if all the gays taking part in that service had left also, the ranks would have looked decidedly thin! I have dared to chide bishops on this.

There is no place in the Kingdom of Love for hatred of gays, nor for any other minority group. Christians, therefore, should support organisations and policies which endeavour to express attitudes of Love for the Creation, and Love for our brothers and sisters. This involves keeping ourselves informed, listening carefully, and trying to evaluate the significance of what we hear.

Evil does not reside only in individuals. It resides also in systems and social relationships. Slavery provided a clear example. A Christian master and a Christian slave could have had genuine affection and respect for each other – but the *relationship* was wrong, and an affront to the gospel. The answer was not to convert as many individual slave-owners as possible and hope for the best. That would have guaranteed nothing. The answer was political action to change society and transform the system. Apartheid, and its evil twin, white supremacy, is another example. Converting enough individuals to new attitudes of justice and compassion will be a long process, with no promise of success at the end. The evil is in the system. The system must be changed.

Some people argue that political systems based upon private property, competition, incentives and personal profits are unchristian, and that greater emphasis on planning, co-operation, common-ownership, and the welfare of the whole community is nearer the spirit of the gospel. Political debate will continue for as long as human beings survive on this planet. But if we are serious in our devotion to Jesus Christ, political involvement becomes not only logical but inevitable, because politics is about the way we treat one another, and because (once again), *politics is the way the world gets changed*.

Of course we can't do everything. We mustn't drop all our church responsibilities. But we must do *something*. To sit in church singing psalms and choruses while others do God's dirty work is not good enough, and will ensure our continued irrelevance. We must get out and across the gap, if it only means joining a party and wearing a badge or delivering a few leaflets. God isn't interested in our prayers if the plight of the world's needy doesn't weigh heavily on our heart. And it's no good admiring a sunset or a symphony if a beaten-up gay or a homeless family doesn't fill you with anger. The harmony is destroyed. You've lost your God. While you're linking him with an impressive building, or a glorious sky, or with sounds which reach out from eternity, Christ is standing in the dole queue, or bleeding in El Salvador.

It is with more pictures of our Lord that I draw this chapter to a close. Perhaps His command to the rich young ruler has an application both wider and sharper than, traditionally, we allow: 'Yet lackest thou one thing: sell all that thou hast, and distribute unto the poor. . .'

Then, in the Sermon on the Mount: 'Lay not up for yourselves treasures upon earth, where moth and rust doth corrupt, and where thieves break through and steal: but lay up for yourselves treasures in heaven . . .' Next follows that curious and lovely phrase: 'For where your treasure is, there will your heart be also.'

Finally, recall the man who, according to Jesus, said: 'I will pull down my barns, and build greater.' To him, God replied: 'Thou fool, this night thy soul shall be required of thee.'

5

The Glory Due unto His Name

Many a working man will smile if you call him names. If you make jokes about the team he supports, he will take it in good part; and if you cast doubts upon his sexual prowess he will laugh and probably agree with you. But should you be reckless enough to criticise his driving, his indignation will be deep, real, and immediate! I have noted a similar reaction among churchpeople. Criticise the effectiveness of our evangelism, or express concern over the quality of our social witness, and people will listen carefully even if they do not agree with what you say. But venture a less than enthusiastic appraisal of modern church worship, and offence may be taken very quickly!

I know, therefore, what reaction to expect. Unfortunately, I can do nothing to prevent it. There is a gulf between the quality of the worship we are tending increasingly to offer, and the perceptions and expectations of those who do not attend church regularly. 'Well, *of course* there is a gap,' some will rejoin. 'Those who do not worship *regularly* cannot expect to understand, and feel instantly at ease.' It is a fair comment, and one I have made in the canteen more than once. But there is more to it than that. This gap is not about *belief*. It is far more serious than that. It is about atmosphere, wonder, spiritual authority, and a sense of holiness. In short, it is about our failure to deliver the goods.

Through no excess of zeal, alas, but by virtue of my employment, I watch a sunrise many times in the course of a year. It never seems boring, or commonplace, or meaningless. Always, I feel that *something is happening*. Sunworship is an ancient practice to which it is easy to relate. A sunrise is intrinsically a religious event: it provokes and stimulates sensations of wonder, splendour, mystery, awe, and reverence. As the great blazing disc lifts itself from the horizon and the light of a new day slants over roof-tops and through the woods, revealing the texture of the bark and the lichen on tree-trunks, it is impossible for any alert and sensitive person to remain unmoved. A new energy radiates through the creation, and the smouldering life of the earth – which has burned low in the darkness – is rekindled, and leaps upwards. Flowers open, birds whistle, men sing. A new heaven and a new earth! New every morning. And as I watch and participate in this daily ritual (usually from my cab, which unfortunately lacks immediacy of contact, rather like watching a church service on television), I can't help thinking: 'How *real* this is. And, by comparison, how *unreal* is so much of our Jesus-talk!'

The universe prompts endless experiences of ecstasy, insight, and intuition – all without benefit of clergy: a sunset, a snowdrop; a cowslip, a motorway kestrel; the face of a friend, a glowing fire; a constellation, a chrysanthemum; a snowflake, a storm cloud; a rainbow, a river; moonlight, and mud. If anyone asks: 'What has a barn owl to do with worship?' I reply: 'It has everything to do with worship.'

Similar revelations are experienced when humankind's creative mind wrestles with, tames and co-operates with the physical elements of the universe to produce new wonders: complex machinery; feats of engineering; computers; television. For many of us, (especially those born before the age of the microchip), the shapes and lines, the designs and materials, which characterised the pioneering craftsmanship of earlier times retain a peculiar potency: a windmill; a farm cart; an historic building; an old bus; a railway steam locomotive. Let no one describe such wonders as lumps of old metal and wood which rot away! At one, mundane level they *are* – but they are incomparably more. They are all expressions of the creativity of the human spirit which wonders, probes, discovers, classifies, harnesses, and struggles to bring order out of chaos. They are testimonies to human endeavour: to that longing to know, to grow, to see beyond, to overcome, to be free. If any should ask: 'What on earth has a steam engine to do with worship?' I reply: 'It has everything to do with worship.'

A plethora of thoughts and emotions are generated as the sun swings, each day, from east to west. Images of human need and suffering appear before us, in the flesh or upon the screen: the hungry, the destitute, the lonely, the sick, the forgotten, and all the innocent victims of man's greed, brutality and degradation. Wonder, fear, anger, pity – our reactions vary, and intermingle. I still remember the vivid impression which one particular television scene of a massacre created in my mind during the Vietnam war. Young men and women lay, face down, on the ground, lifeless. Breasts and buttocks which should have heaved and fallen in the extravagances of passion lay still and sunken. I recall, in addition to the sense of horror and revulsion, a deep feeling of heaviness at the thought of such appalling *waste*. Human bodies are sacred and mysterious. 'I am fearfully and wonderfully made', said the psalmist; 'With my body I thee worship,' says the bridegroom. The bodies of tiny babies . . . the fast-growing bodies of children . . . the attractive, energetic bodies of young men and women . . . the strong, mature bodies of those in middle years . . . the bodies of the old, gnarled with experience and beautiful in fulfilment . . . Should any dare ask: 'What has a hungry child to do with worship?' I would disdain to answer. But if one should ask: 'What has the human form to do with worship?' I answer, again, 'Everything!'

'Put off thy shoes from off thy feet, for the place where-
on thou standest is holy ground.' We should, perhaps, go
shoeless all the time, for every place, every moment, every
person, and every circumstance carries within it the possibility of an encounter with the Divine. These encounters
– these experiences of insight and intuition, revelation and
recognition – can be deeply moving and, sometimes, even
painful in their intensity. (A swan which glided unexpec-
tedly into view as I stood admiring a peaceful river scene
one summer's evening, almost destroyed me.) But, for the
most part, they cannot be timed, planned, or engineered.
They cannot be fixed for 10.45 a.m. They are the spontaneous products of daily life, regulated by the round of
the seasons. By contrast, acts of worship performed in
church are set-piece activities, fixed, of necessity, at a certain hour. In these we attempt, deliberately, to respond to
The Mystery: to the God who, we believe, sustains the
whole creation from moment to moment, and is revealed
within it. That is why an essentially informal – and, occasionally, even casual – approach to public worship fails to
satisfy me, and (on the few occasions they come into contact with it) does nothing for people like my workmates. It
produces an atmosphere *which sags beneath the level of wonder and sheer spiritual reality induced by the creation itself.*

Going to church can be an incredible anti-climax. There
is within the creation Unity in Diversity and Diversity in
Unity. There is an essential harmony with which our worship needs to blend, if it is to ring true. There is nothing
flippant about the cosmos; nothing trivial. The creatures
possess a natural dignity and gracefulness. The creation
displays beauty and power, energy and joy, pain and horror, orderliness and spontaneity: *but it never embarrasses.*
The creation is a kaleidoscope of colour, sound, light, and
movement; and these should find reflection in our
worship.

In church services, therefore, I look first for dignity, reverence, awe, and a sense of otherness. I do not look for cold formality, nor for pompous, artificial theatricality, but for that quiet, purposeful, natural bearing which becomes a creature deliberately reminding itself of, and attempting to realise, the presence of its Creator. I look, secondly, for warmth: not over-familiarity with holy things; not gushing sentimentality, nor hearty chumminess; not that *false* appeal to the emotions which does dirt on people's real feelings; but I look for a deep sense of mutual acceptance, for better for worse; for a sense of 'belonging', for the ever-present hint of laughter; for the simple, uncomplicated humanity of a loving community. Those whose attendance at worship is infrequent are not impervious to this combination. The holiness silences them; the humanity warms them.

The myth which we employ to interpret our experience of existence is the beautiful, ever-contemporary, ever-searching, ever-tantalising, ever-true story of Jesus Christ. We proclaim that He came from the galactic centre of the universe, from the blaze of uncreated light beyond all space and time, to reveal its meaning and its secret: that the creation is an expression of Love, and is upheld by Love. To live in harmony with the creation means – for creatures with our abilities – to live in Love. To be part of a worshipping community should mean hearing about, experiencing, sharing, and imparting the Love which moves through all things. This vision of the Cosmic Christ lies at the heart of Christian worship:

> The voice that rolls the stars along
> Speaks all the promises.

There is an important passage in the Sermon on the Mount about bringing a gift to the altar of God and then remembering the existence of a wrong relationship between yourself and another. 'Go, first, and try to put that matter right,' we are told. 'Then come and worship!' The implications which flow from those words are far-reaching indeed. Worship is important. But righteousness comes first – that love for our neighbour which means justice and peace, caring and sharing, forgiveness and up-rightness, brotherhood and sisterhood, the guiding principle of the family, the analogy of the team – all the things we considered in the previous chapter. It's a wonder that the prayers we offer don't choke us . . .

The shape and content of our liturgy are, primarily, matters of personal preference. We may assume that God enjoys our hymn-singing, and appreciates the effort and the discipline which produces excellence in composition and performance. But the hymns, prayers, and lessons are important *in themselves* chiefly for the effects they have upon *us*: for the spiritual and emotional realities they enable us to express, and the vision, commitment, and dedication they inspire. God looks for sincerity. The form of our services matters only in so far as it enables us to offer our noblest worship, and express our loftiest thoughts. 'They that worship Him must worship Him in spirit and in truth.'

I am not, therefore, about to suggest arrogantly that those whose approach to worship differs from my own are making an inferior offering, unacceptable to Almighty God. His first requirement is that we should do justly, love mercy, and walk humbly with our God. Then He looks for sincerity in our worship. Then He looks for our best – however humble and faltering and imperfect our best might be.

At this point, I can no longer postpone answering some questions I would have preferred to avoid. Why has churchgoing become something of an effort for me? Why do I share so many of the attitudes to worship held by non-churchgoers? Why am I disillusioned? Why am I angry (because I *am* angry)? Looking in from outside, I am depressed by the quality of our worship. For nearly a quarter of a century I have been endeavouring to witness to the Love of God at the centre of the rough-and-tumble of the world's everyday life. Now – to be honest – in my worst moments, I feel that while I have been out there concentrating on the battle, I find that – behind my back – people have been busy ruining the services!

In H.E. Bates' delightful short story, *Oh! Sweeter than the Berry*, the eccentric Miss Shuttleworth receives a pastoral visit from the Reverend H. Sloane Arrowsmith, who mellows progressively with each glass of her home-made wine. His hostess chatters incessantly:

> 'By the way,' Miss Shuttleworth said, entirely and irrepressibly changing the subject, 'there was something I wanted to ask you. Of course I don't attend church service regularly but only at christenings, weddings and funerals. But tell me this. Why have you gone and mucked about with the Lord's Prayer?'
>
> 'But have we? I wasn't aware –'
>
> 'Appallingly and illogically balled it up.' Miss Shuttleworth fortified herself with a good deep draught of cherry brandy, at the same time taking the opportunity to replenish Mr Arrowsmith's glass. Mr Arrowsmith, slightly pained by the thought that the church had mucked up the Lord's Prayer, hardly noticed and had no word of protest.
>
> 'Mucked it up. Good and proper. And shall I tell you how? . . .'
>
> 'Miss Shuttleworth, I think there are cogent reasons –'
>
> 'There'd better be. Good, solid, logical ones too. And do you use that appalling modern version of the New Testament?'
>
> 'Yes, we do.'

'Codswallop. Reads like a batch of Urban Council Minutes from the backwoods somewhere.

'Miss Shuttleworth, I think perhaps I ought to be trotting along –'

'You know what that wretched version needs? A drop of this. A drop of wine in its shaky soul and bones.'

I think I would get on well with Miss Shuttleworth. I share her prejudices. To me, the voluntary surrender of the traditional version of the Lord's Prayer, once known to saints and sinners alike, was a disastrous own-goal. We are producing, now, a nation unable to recite any prayer at all. I feel strongly that we would find it helpful if a clear – though not rigid – distinction could be made between 'fellowship' and 'worship' – between groups meeting for prayer and bible study (perhaps in somebody's home), and public services conducted in church.

Fellowship can soar into worship; and Christian worship which does not create a sense of fellowship is defective. Yet these two means of grace are different, and some ingredients which may enhance fellowship may not 'work' so effectively in worship. Sweeping liturgical changes have been made in recent years; clocks cannot be put back, even if we wanted. I am trying, therefore, to select my words carefully, because my criticism of modern worship goes deeper than arguments over rites and versions. It concerns the relaxed approach which has evolved – and the lack of atmosphere and 'absence of any sense of occasion' which has resulted. However, I will confess that, for me, the Authorised Version, and 'thee' rather than 'you', still has a place in contemporary worship. Over the centuries, the AV has sunk deep into the national consciousness – it is part of our history, our language, our literature – and I see nothing wrong in having a distinctive form of language available to help convey, in this curious age, a realisation of the holy. Too much modern worship is 'fellowship-orientated'; too little conveys 'The speechless awe that dares not move'.

I have observed that some of the clamour to use 'the language of the market-place' in worship has come from people who seldom visit the market-place. Here, again, is evidence of the gap. I live in the market-place, and I don't want to hear its language when I visit the house of God for rest and refreshment, for contemplation and worship. Just as we have preserved *Kyrie eleison*, we should have seen the even greater wisdom of shamelessly putting a fence around the old form of the Lord's Prayer – and extending the principle to include some of the other high points of Christian devotion to which the years have given a widely-acknowledged authenticity, like the *Ave Maria*.

After being active in the life of the church since I was a teenager, I find myself, now, depressed beyond words by the modern service books and the new hymnals which accompany them. When the tools for the job are defective, the most skilled craftsman will struggle. Worship is not an exact science; it relies upon poetry and poetic images. Yet we have become almost prudish in our susceptibilities! Phrases like 'in this vale of misery' are viewed with suspicion and likely to be dropped – despite the fact that it is a perfect description of what life is like for all of us, sometimes, and for millions all the time. My own denomination produced a new hymn book a few years ago, and I was disappointed by the large number of *trivial* changes made to well-known tunes and words. Far from being an improvement, such casually-introduced amendments have serious repercussions. They impair the sense of reassurance which comes from uttering familiar words and notes, and the sense of 'belonging' which comes from doing it together. They also harm the subtle nuances which contribute so much to the impact of worship. The tune is often as important as the words, and small, unexpected changes to either can jar disastrously. The fact that these objections have to be spelled out is, perhaps, in itself revealing.

The Wesley hymns form part of the distinctive core of my church's worshipping tradition, but several of the very best were deleted from the new book. The hymns of John and Charles Wesley possess a timeless quality which always enhances worship – for reasons Colin Morris has described:

> We can sing beyond our conscious, debatable beliefs because the healthy ambiguities of meaning in poetry and music allow room for that wistful agnosticism which is a salutary attitude when confronting a God who is by definition unknowable. Being beyond the range of the senses, He is more likely to haunt our imaginations than rest easily in our logic-chopping propositions. Thanks to their supreme minstrel, the Methodist people have never been deprived of luminous images in which to enshrine their deepest experiences. He has left no central doctrines unexplored; no profound spiritual depths uncharted. Charles Wesley's hymns have fired my imagination, fuelled my preaching, sustained my prayer life, and given me a comprehensive plan of salvation I could both commend to others and follow gratefully myself.

All the major denominations have revised their liturgies and produced similar results. If the end-product gives you little delight, there are no hiding-places. We're in this together. Ironically, we have done it to further the mission of the church – to make worship more intelligible and meaningful, especially to people like those with whom I work. Our motives were beyond reproach – yet, somehow, we lost our way; *and thousands of us know it, in our heart of hearts.* But we don't know what to do about it. The simple, galling truth is that Britain is not a virgin mission field. It is something far more complex, where nearly two thousand years of history and tradition are at once cherished and rejected in a weird mixture of faith and unbelief. Those who worship only rarely, *expect* to hear the authentic, familiar words when they take the trouble to join us, and are nowhere near so distressed as we pretend to hear some 'archaic' expressions – if their effect is not to obscure, but to heighten a sense of worship and wonder.

At the popular midnight mass held in many churches on Christmas Eve, the clergy can scarcely go wrong. It is a night of friendship, wonder, warmth and expectancy, when our myth is at its most powerful and persuasive. Bathed in that heady atmosphere; supported by the strange lateness of the hour, the seasonal decorations, and the barely-suppressed excitement; crowned with the beauty and irresistible appeal of the Christmas story – the minister has only to repeat the traditional words in Scripture and liturgy, and preach simply and briefly. The occasion carries *itself* along.

Yet I have been to midnight eucharists which, *for me*, have been defused and neutralised by the modern rite. It worked no spell. *The magic in the air was greater than that in the liturgy*; the words failed to match and channel the mood, and the people became restless, and many slipped away to find taxis . . . If you can produce that effect on Christmas Eve, when all the cards are in your hand, there is no room for complacency.

Let us keep our liturgies and forms of service under constant review, but let us also be humbly aware that among all the astonishing blessings given to this generation, the gift of powerful liturgical language appears – for the most part – to have been withheld. When changes and revisions become necessary, it is vital that they be done well. 'Quench not the Spirit'; but 'let everything be done decently and in order.' Old-fashioned language can be as off-putting as modern prose. I use a new translation of the Bible when I believe it will help to make God more real and less remote. That is the test. I exult in my Free Church freedom to arrange worship in whatever ways I deem most seemly and appropriate – even if this results in an unconventional mix of churchmanship. But it must be the *best* I can offer. In worship, the second-rate has no place. It has crept in – the third- and fourth-rate with it.

Throughout this chapter, my gaze has continued to be fixed on the gap. What we do for our own satisfaction is one thing, but when we make the task of evangelism even more difficult, that is another. Each time I conduct an act of public worship, I ask myself what a non-churchgoer would make of it, if he or she had happened, by chance, to be present. I would not expect them, at the end, to be ready to give general assent to the Thirty-Nine Articles, but I would hope they had not been too embarassed by their experience; that they had recognised a certain validity in the proceedings and agreed with a few of the sentiments expressed; that they felt I had played my role in the production in a dignified yet human fashion; and that it wouldn't be the end of the world if they were forced to come again, some time. I would like much, much more! But I recognise the point from which we start and the distance we have to travel.

Upon those responsible for the conduct of public worship – ministers and lay preachers – lies an enormous responsibility. Sometimes, our bearing does not suggest that we are conscious of being engaged in one of the most lofty and awesome of all human activities: leading men and women into the closer presence of their Maker and in the worship of their God. There is no sense of drama. I emphasise, again, that I am not pleading for affected histrionics; still less for pomposity; nothing could be more distracting or inappropriate. But quiet reverence, stillness which springs from spiritual depths, care over details, dignity in movement, and single-minded attentiveness to the unique task in hand are not optional extras.

The atmosphere in worship should not lag impossibly behind those experiences of 'otherness' with which we are familiar in other areas of life – which are provoked by the wonder and beauty of nature; by the mysteriousness of sex and love; by the strange, translucent quality of our intuitions and visions; by the darkness of our moments of terror; by the delight of our music, literature, poetry, and simpler pleasures – even, perhaps, our sport. It is here our worship is failing, and it is failing – in part – because those responsible for its conduct are not always 'professional' enough. We are sensitive to the glory of the creation; we are warmed by friendship, thrilled by love; we are appalled by pain and ugliness; we think deep thoughts . . . Then we go into church and offer worship which is a disgrace to the cosmos! It is not ruined by heresy. It is ruined by the absence of any sense of occasion.

This book is not intended solely for preachers, so I must not pause at this point *too* long. I must, however, mention a few matters which seem, to me, to be important if we believe that worship is not only for the committed and converted, but is also – still – a primary form of evangelism. They are, in themselves, small matters – but they can ruin the play, the drama, the peep-show into eternity which we call worship.

The entry of the minister into the church should be the equivalent of curtain-up at the theatre or the entry of the judge into the courtroom: the long-awaited moment of promise and expectation; the beginning. (If he has not been standing about and chatting in the church before the service begins, so much the better. And even if you are visualising a tiny, one-roomed village chapel, *the principle is the same*: the service starts when the preacher stands, and a great deal hangs on the first words uttered.) The importance of this initial quiet dignity and reverence, which sets the scene for all that is to follow, cannot be exaggerated. From the outset, the dramatic advantage lies with the minister. How frequently and casually that advantage is thrown away!

The most obvious illustration of this particular form of insensitivity occurs regularly at weddings, and has direct relevance to the gap. Services of holy matrimony provide a rich combination of factors which never fail to engender an atmosphere of expectancy. Usually, there is a large congregation. (A full house is always exciting!) Most of those present are not regular worshippers and, consequently, are self-conscious and slightly ill-at-ease. They are, therefore, at a disadvantage emotionally – they are receptive, and *waiting* to be told what to do. Above all, of course, they are waiting for an event – for the arrival and dramatic entry of the bride. The bride, unfailingly, plays her part by traditionally arriving a little late – and every second she can steal heightens the tension, till it becomes almost unbearable, and delicious! At last, she arrives! A car door slams, feet shuffle in the church porch (but a different kind of shuffling from that heard at funerals), and the great moment is at hand. What will her dress be like? (Will her father be sober?) The organ blares out the familiar notes for which everyone has been waiting. The bridal party enters the church, walks slowly through the assembled company, and joins the bridegroom before the priest. The music stops. All eyes switch to the man of God. It is his move next. Will his opening lines be sentences of Scripture? or the announcement, perhaps, of the opening hymn, which will give everyone a chance to drink deeply of this potent atmosphere while – at the same time

– settling down? Possibly. The opening word from the Lord, however, is often less inspiring. 'I must ask you to refrain from throwing confetti until the bride and groom have left the churchyard. It makes such an awful mess and . . .' It doesn't matter if it's a reference to the plate at the back of the church, or an awkward word of welcome. With one false move he has surrendered every ace he held, and reduced the atmosphere to that of any other meeting. He may recover some ground as the service proceeds, but nothing will compensate for having failed to take advantage of that all-important opening moment. For once, I have not sketched a caricature. The kind of gross insensitivity and incompetence to which I refer is encountered all too often.

As worship begins, the attention of the person responsible for its conduct should be fixed upon his holy duty and sensitive to the prevailing atmosphere, ready to seize upon it and direct it and use it. Thoughts of confetti, collections, and greeting can wait. We are entering the Divine Presence. When a minister or preacher enters the church, or climbs into the pulpit, it is as the representative of Jesus Christ. This most awesome joy and privilege embraces the cosmic dimension of our faith. He (or she) represents the Man of Nazareth *and* the Cosmic Christ, by whom all things were created, and by whom all things consist. He represents, therefore, the sunrise, he represents Orion, he represents the whale and the osprey, he represents the twin principles of masculinity and femininity around which the earth revolves, he represents the God who is somehow involved in the blood of road accidents and the emaciation of cancer. That is the background against which priesthood, ministry, and preaching are set. That is its ultimate context. And that is why the trivial, the trite, and the mundane have no place in Christian worship.

The lack of 'professionalism' results in the spell of worship being broken, and the sense of otherness dissipated. Those responsible for the conduct of worship should not wander about during the service more than is absolutely necessary. Handing out hymn books, switching on lights, and similar errands are distractions. Imagine Sir Toby Belch breaking off in mid-speech to sell a couple of programmes or to distribute ice-creams in the auditorium! The illusion would be shattered, and the production would flounder in an air of unreality. Similarly, every movement and gesture in worship should have significance. There are, of course, no hard and fast rules, but extraneous movements should be kept to an absolute minimum.

An element of objectivity and detachment in the attitude of the person conducting worship is essential. Priests who regularly broke down during funerals, or were more nervous than the bride during weddings, would not be very effective. But it is a terrible thing when the person set apart to lead the worship of God shows *the wrong kind of 'professionalism'* and comes near to conveying the impression that, to him, it's just a job. A young chorister said to me after a service: 'I wish he would wait a minute at the end of the anthem before switching on the microphone and starting the prayers . . .' I was impressed by his childish perception, and knew at once what had provoked the comment. A sublime anthem, beautifully rendered, had moved the entire congregation, recapturing their wandering thoughts and turning their minds toward the God of their salvation. As the last notes faded, a spirit of peace and aspiration filled the church. It was worship pure and holy – worship to be savoured and offered for a few more deliberate, fleeting seconds. The opportunity was not given. Before the echo died away, a microphone crackled into life and a voice snapped, 'Let us pray.' We fell back to

earth with a crash! Had this man been totally unaffected
by what had just happened? Did *he* not need time to swal-
low hard, and shake off the overwhelming beauty? Appar-
ently not. Needless to say, the prayers that followed
neither maintained nor restored the beauty which had
been destroyed.

Trivial, tell-tale incidents like these cause me distress,
because they turn acts of living worship which just *might*
have had some connection with Ultimate Reality into
empty charades. Those who attend church regularly may
become accustomed to worship which is presented poorly,
but people dragged in from across the gap are on foreign
soil and, therefore, more alert; they sense it immediately. I
want nothing false or over-elaborate – only careful attention and a natural dignity in the conduct of worship, be it
in city cathedral or country chapel.

To see a yellow wagtail in the full brilliance of its spring
plumage you must find one in April, soon after its arrival
from Africa, before the colours become dulled by the wear
and tear of the breeding season. One year I saw my first on
16th April. I was walking by the river when suddenly I
noticed it, standing in the grass only yards from my feet. I
know that I gave an audible gasp of pleasure, surprise,
wonder and joy, stunned by the small creature's exquisite
beauty. I could not drag myself away, but simply stood
staring, for many minutes. When, at last, it flew off across
the marsh, I was almost relieved, for I could not possibly
have left it. I was under a kind of spell. My spontaneous
reaction that day contained many of the basic ingredients
of true worship: the surprise, reverence, awe, mystery,
wonder; the sense of one-ness. Worshipping is a human
activity as natural as eating, drinking, and making love.
What happens in church must be related to experiences
like my meeting with the first yellow wagtail of spring.
When there *is* no connection, I am left wishing – with all

my heart – that I had opted for a seat in the pub, an hour with my records, or a walk on the heath.

Worship should heighten, intensify and concentrate something which is already present in the mystery of existence, the wonder of creation, and the beauty of love. Our worship should be grounded in our experience of the Trinity, offering reverence for The Mystery, love for The Love, and openness to the renewing, energising, transforming Power. In an ever-changing world, it should convey a sense of permanence, and in a world largely given over to the transient pursuits of Time, a sense of Eternity.

One of the aims of modern mission – more significant, in this generation, than the inculcation of a particular emotional experience, or even the winning of intellectual assent – is to enable people to worship. Humankind *needs* the experience of worship, and finds fulfilment in acknowledging the vital, enriching dimensions of mystery, wonder, and otherness – when opportunities arise to do so corporately and unselfconsciously. We are impoverished if we do not worship. In one sense, it is *worse* than being under-nourished, or having nobody to love. Something at the very centre of what it means to be a human being begins to die.

I am convinced that the worshipping faculty has by no means been destroyed among the 90 per cent who seldom enter a church, but it has become encrusted, enfeebled, and diverted. (There is never any shortage of alternative gods.) Some, of course, deplore its continued existence, and view it as an unhealthy, subservient trait which, at this stage of evolution, we should have outgrown. Not surprisingly, I am unmoved by this attitude, and reject the spirit of pride I detect at its heart: the arrogance of creature man; the arrogance of Adam and Eve, who wanted to know as only God can know. In Christian thought, 'sin' is not only a falling-away from our nature at its noblest and best; it also means climbing high, and proudly attempting to exceed our rightful place in the universe, managing without reference to God, and forgetting to worship.

When people are lured into a church to participate, however vaguely, in a Christian service, they should be exposed to wonder and worship. They should find themselves bathed in an atmosphere which differs, indefinably, from home, work, pub, or any other familiar environment – yet which is not uncongenial; indeed, it should seem to half-remind them of something they cannot, for the moment, quite recall. Secretly, I suspect that – if I were not already within the fellowship of the church – it is unlikely that the services today (in church or chapel) would win me.

Mission in modern Britain, where centuries of Christian tradition go hand-in-hand with widespread indifference to routine churchgoing, has to operate at two levels which – in practice – must overlap, but in our thinking ought, probably, to be kept apart. When social custom or residual faith demands a religious ceremony – *and such requests should always delight us* – we have to create, provide and make real a sense of otherness which people can recognise and to which they can relate and respond. This means providing 'folk religion', particularly for the rites of passage, *and doing it well*. We shall be able to discharge this obligation with a clear conscience once we allow it to sink into our heads that *God loves all the people all the time* – not just the confirmed or 'saved' ones, some of the time. If, as I have argued, it is natural for men and women to worship, I would ten thousand times rather that their worship (such as it is) be directed to the God and Father of Our Lord Jesus Christ – who *is* their Maker, and their Lover, and their Lord – rather than to the false gods we are so adept at fashioning in our own image. (Incidentally, the quality of their offering will be linked to our own enabling skills.) This will be the subject of the next chapter.

Our other responsibility is, I hope, obvious. In our worship we have to praise and point to Jesus, the Light of the World; to proclaim His Kingdom of Love; to extol Him as the Way, the Truth, and the Life; to endeavour to make new Christians; and to build each other up in the Faith. For me, however, all these tasks are linked inevitably with the tone, the content, and the quality of our worship. Worship *at its best* still bridges the gap – when people can be persuaded to try it. Speak about Jesus against a background of super-simple liturgy, with an absolute minimum of formality, and you will be lucky to cut any ice. People will look blank; some of the most sensitive will cringe. The world of Sunday car-cleaning, the world of work, the world of the pub and the club are light years away from what is being offered, increasingly, in many churches. But speak about Jesus, quietly and naturally – the Jesus 'who told us we should be kind to each other, and care about each other, and should try to build a world where there are no wars and no starving people' – and do it in an atmosphere unashamedly *different*, generated by a sensitive and judicious selection of traditional and familiar material, laced modestly (where possible) with simple features of catholic devotion (like candles) which have universal appeal (because humankind is essentially catholic at heart), and you just *could* be in with a chance. (It is worthy of note that, since catholic devotion is highly visual, it has been portrayed in countless films throughout this century, and thus acquired a reinforced authenticity we are foolish to ignore. Nothing which, with imagination, could be pressed into the service of the gospel should be dismissed out of hand – as the next chapter, I hope, will make plain.)

Despite the world's continuing unbelief, the intellectual climate has changed in recent years, and attitudes have shifted. We are losing less ground for 'intellectual' reasons – but we are still losing it through the quality of our worship, and this slow, relentless haemorrhage is sapping our spiritual strength. For many thoughtful people, concerts and the countryside offer far more satisfying fare – an either/or situation we should never have allowed to develop. We have done for worship what commercialisation has done for sex. We have destroyed the mystery. I don't want universal Latin or compulsory 1662 any more than I want to see ankles covered again, or jeans made less tight! However, the mystery to which I refer is part of the very essence of sexuality and of religion. It stimulates the reverence without which both become hollow, cheap, and – often – nasty. That bitter discovery is one of the great tragedies of life in Britain today. The ultimate paradox, for human beings, is that there is no meaning without mystery.

In one matter, as in no other, I have the certainty of the martyr! Even if I stand alone, nothing will ever shake this conviction. I recognise that tremendous energy and commitment have gone into the revision of our worship, and countless thousands are grateful. So be it! But we have settled for the easy option. Getting into the world, and staying there for God; accepting a comparatively poor and simple way of life, and acknowledging the inescapability of political involvement – these cost far, far more. So new hymn books, new service books, and new Bibles have proliferated; but, for *me*, we've come near to throwing out the baby with the bath water. When I come in from the world, bruised, bloodied, and exhausted, I cry out only for worship in which I may be 'lost in wonder, love, and praise.'

Yet when I ask for bread, I am given a stone; when I ask for fish, a serpent. And in my disappointment, I turn sadly away, and retreat across the gap to search for crumbs of vision and inspiration in the world.

> Almighty God, to Thee
>   Be endless honours done,
> The undivided Three,
>   And the mysterious One.
> Where reason fails, with all her powers,
> There faith prevails and love adores.

6

The Bells of St Clement's

Early one Saturday evening, as I walked past a cricket field on my way home from a wedding reception, I was delighted to see that a match was in progress. I stayed for almost an hour, watching with what I can only describe as approval. I enjoy cricket, but I am not a fanatic – and certainly never played with any flair or natural talent. Yet there was a curious 'rightness' about the scene before me, which appealed. Cricket pitches *ought* to have matches played on them at the week-end in summer. The sound of leather against willow is somehow reassuring – and very English! The fact that the names of the various fielding positions, and all the other technical terms, mystify me completely, didn't matter. A game was in progress. An empty field would have left me poorer. I would have noticed – and regretted that part of our diverse common heritage appeared neglected and uncherished. I never play, and seldom watch. I rely on others to keep the tradition alive. Then I am glad – and grateful.

As a well-struck ball raced towards the boundary, it occurred to me that a close parallel probably existed between my attitude to the cricket I was watching, and the cricketers' attitude to churches and churchgoing. People like to see churches: they are a familiar and reassuring feature of the landscape in both town and country. People are easily hurt and affronted when churches fall into disrepair, or are closed, or demolished. They like to feel that services are still being held in the churches – that prayers are being said, and hymns sung. If the language is somewhat dated – perhaps even bewildering – it doesn't matter very much. Indeed, it's what they expect. They themselves seldom attend, though they might make an effort at Christmas or Harvest, given a push. For the most part, they rely on others to keep the tradition alive – and often admire the dedication of those who do so.

The parallel amused me, and I chuckled aloud. (Perhaps my insight was not unrelated to the hospitality I had enjoyed at the reception!) They were playing cricket *for me*! I had watched for a while, and derived enjoyment and satisfaction. (And they were doing it properly, *in the way I expected*: they were not dressed in tartan flannels, or using a tennis ball.) Tomorrow, I would go to church *for them*. Some of them would join me, one week, at the christening or on Easter Day – in much the same way as I had shared a few overs with them – and I hoped they would derive similar benefit. But they would not be coming to every 'match'. It is, however, in this manner that our common life is shared. We each have specific functions and particular interests, yet remain members one of another. Obviously, there is much overlapping. You *can* go to church *and* play cricket. But, in practice, nobody does everything, and a division of responsibilities is not only unavoidable, but a mark of the rich diversity of human society. We are right to maintain that religion should figure prominently in the lives of all, and right to be appalled by the gap and by the degree to which religion has become a minority interest. Yet the fact remains that the duty of giving practical support to the church, and the obligation to bear witness to the Faith, are likely always to fall upon a minority. The majority are surprisingly willing to help, if their interest can be awakened – in the same way that I purchased some raffle tickets to support the cricket club. But the main burden rests upon the few in the preservation of holy places and the provision of rites and ceremonies. We do it for the health of our own souls; but we should do it, above all, for the benefit of the community.

When our neighbours are so moved as to require religion for the adequate expression of their experiences, *we should be able to supply it* – and in a form and language which captures their aspirations at the flood and carries them forward to new levels of understanding and fulfilment. Perhaps it *is* 'folk religion', but it is none the worse for that; I enjoyed my 'folk cricket'. Whatever we believe we have to offer men and women, it must be pitched at the level where they live and move and have their being. It must capture their intuitive awareness of mystery and the regular passage of time. To people who have forgotten or have never known them, our cherished doctrines must often be introduced along the lines I tried to indicate in chapter Two. ('Crucifixion is about what we do to love . . .'). But that need never preclude our fulfilling the injunction of the Scotswoman to her young nephew on the eve of his first sermon in his first church: '. . . But, oh, laddie, be sure ye say a gude word for Jesus Christ.'

One of the facets of my unconventional ministry for which I am most grateful is the unique opportunity I have been given to become a purveyor of high-quality folk religion. As a catholic-spirited nonconformist, I have exploited this singular privilege to the utmost, and have gleaned from it almost as much as I have learned from the more visible and swashbuckling aspects of ministry in the bus garage and on the city streets. The two things, however, go together.

The city in which I was born and where I have spent most of my life possesses the largest collection of medieval churches in western Europe. The majority have been declared redundant, and for many years I have been permitted to hire the ancient church of St Clement, and have opened it daily as a place of sanctuary and prayer. The site is undoubtedly Saxon. Prayer has been offered and the sacraments celebrated here for over a thousand years. The church is simple and plain, but it occupies a corner site in the centre of the city and at night is dramatically floodlit.

St Clement's has an aisleless chancel and a wide aisleless nave, which was in the process of being enlarged by the parish when the Return of Church Goods was compiled in 1552. Beside the pulpit is a blocked arch, which provides an interesting reminder of the English Reformation. It was intended as the entrance to the rood turret, but roods were banned early in the reign of Edward VI, just at the time the nave of St Clement's was under reconstruction. Plans had to be amended, leaving behind an archway which never led anywhere – like many people's religion! The post-Reformation roof is totally devoid of decoration or religious imagery, and the church has a slim west tower with three bells. St Clement's Church is noted also for its good collection of mural monuments. Over the years, I have discovered that non-churchgoers are not insensitive to the history, architecture and atmosphere of old churches, particularly when interesting features are drawn to their attention and explained. It is not difficult to press history into the service of the gospel.

As I lived opposite St Clement's and had long treasured its tranquillity, the prospect of seeing it adapted for commercial use saddened me. It was like abandoning an old friend (apart from the fact that I was losing one of the chief sources of my spiritual energy). I approached a few people – like the local publican – to inquire if we could raise enough money each year to retain the church in its existing form, and so it proved. The church reopened, not to house a new sect or to compete with other churches in the area (most of which are necessarily kept locked), but simply to offer stillness and quiet. As a redundant church, it boasted no congregation, but it has provided a base for my worker-priest ministry where I have been able to offer counsel, and to arrange occasional services when occasion demanded.

I began my ministry amid the excitement of the Anglican-Methodist Unity Conversations, only to be cruelly disappointed at the outcome, which I still believe to have been a disaster. I vowed that narrow denominationalism would play no part in my ministry. Our divisions carry little weight across the gap (except in abnormal situations like Northern Ireland). I have, therefore, always claimed everything good in the history of the Christian church, from whatever source, as my heritage. This ecumenical and catholic spirit has found expression at St Clement's. The 'education' I myself received through having a son in a cathedral choir, and the experience I gained in a team ministry (before the arrival of *The Alternative Service Book!*), also contributed to my brand of churchmanship and my liturgical dexterity. Denominations *impoverish* us. There is so much inspiring material available to help us see God more clearly, but our divisions mean that we tend to be familiar with only a fraction of it.

At St Clement's, I have felt able to draw on the best resources available for the needs of any given set of circumstances. A mediaeval church building has been a tremendous advantage, providing ideal test conditions for the dispensing of folk religion. It fulfils most people's traditional idea of what a church should look like. (Folk religion, however, can be celebrated anywhere.) Having no resident congregation has tended to be an advantage in ministering to people from across the gap. I have not had to look anxiously over my shoulder to avoid offending the faithful in my attempts to win the 'other sheep' to whom Jesus referred, 'which are not of this fold' but for whom He cares with a tenderness equal to that He shows towards us. There are, however, far more disadvantages. Nobody to pray for me, no loving fellowship into which to introduce people in need of tender support, no one to dust and clean, play the organ, prepare the church, clear away after services, or do *anything*. Fortunately, the services are not very frequent!

St Clement's has one outstanding attribute which many casual visitors – of all types – have sensed and commented upon: 'It has a lovely atmosphere', they say. And they are right!

> An atmosphere of awe and mystery;
> A vivid, strange intensity of space;
> An energy, a power, a potency
> So almost tangible! a holy place!
> Not every famous church these secrets share!
> In plain, forgotten churches – God is there . . .

Those lines are taken from a long poem entitled 'The City of Churches', in which I had my own church very much in mind:

> Saint Clement at Fye Bridge waits modestly,
> And, through the darkness, watches for the dawn;
> It boasts no aisle, no lofty clerestory,
> Yet warmth imparts, in which new hopes are born;
> When daylight falls upon its slender tower,
> The church is filled with vibrant, mystic power.
>
> At evening, too, a curious peace descends,
> Which soothes the stress and passion of the day;
> The line dividing past and present ends,
> And mid-day certainties soon flee away . . .
> In spirit, past parishioners appear:
> Amid the shadows, softly they draw near . . .

Quiet contemplation is not difficult in such an environment. It is here, so often, I have thought of old Père Chaffangeon, who – as everybody knows - used to remain for hours before the altar in the church at Ars, without even moving his lips. He was speaking to God.

'And what do you say to Him?' the Curé asked.

'Oh', replied the old peasant, 'He looks at me, and I look at Him.'

I have found St Clement's a good place to sit and look at God.

Yet however attractive, and however congenial the atmosphere, a redundant church can still seem *bare* without the tell-tale signs of everyday life scattered about. To help counteract this bareness, I have introduced a handful of features to make the building feel and look lived-in. A small statue of our Lady of Walsingham reminds visitors of the Blessed Virgin Mary, the contemplation of whose loving obedience seems, always, to produce great joy. A stoup filled with holy water from Walsingham enables people to reaffirm their baptism, and to pray: 'Wash me throughly from mine iniquity, and cleanse me from my sin . . . Wash me, and I shall be whiter than snow . . .' Votive candles are available, because few things give me greater joy than to enter the church and find a candle burning. It tells me that, in a world of much darkness, someone has had faith enough to say a prayer and light a flame of hope and witness. The psychological and spiritual impact of lighting a candle for a person who is sick, or departed, or in special need, or simply whom you love, is powerful and strangely comforting. I always feel that, somehow, it makes my prayer visible and tangible, and thus both reinforces and prolongs its efficacy. Some find such musings crude and objectionable, but I believe that to remember a person, and to light a candle for them, is to support them, wherever they are, in an almost practical manner. I cannot explain the mechanics of it, but I sense that something good and positive happens. (Across the gap, this kind of devotion passes without adverse comment – indeed, is sometimes accepted gratefully – on the grounds that if you insist on believing in God, it is only reasonable to assume that He is within reach, and will respond and actually *do* things.)

On the wall of St Clement's is displayed the first banner of my busworkers' trade union branch. This is an acknowledgement of the generous annual donation the branch makes to the church. If battle colours can be laid up in a cathedral, a trade union banner can rest honourably in a redundant church. Nearby is a picture of John Wesley, the founder of my own branch of the Christian church, and the author of that remarkable sermon on 'Catholic Spirit', which ought to be more widely known:

> Is thine heart right, as my heart is with thy heart? . . . If it be, give me thine hand: I do not mean, 'Be of my opinion.' You need not: I do not expect or desire it . . . I do not mean, 'Embrace my modes of worship'; or, 'I will embrace yours.' This also is a thing which does not depend either on your choice or mine. We must both act as each is fully persuaded in his own mind . . . I mean, love me . . .

Copies of my edited version of the eucharistic hymns of John and Charles Wesley, entitled *The Richest Legacy*, are available for use in St Clement's. These hymns form an incomparable treasure-house of devotional material, whose scandalous neglect I am determined to end by making them readily available again.

Often, a sanctuary lamp is kept burning before the altar – an instant reminder of the Divine presence – and I like to display an ikon in the church, but these tend to get stolen very quickly. (Poor St Clement's! It possesses little of value, and is open to all every day – yet it is robbed, burgled, or used as a toilet regularly. Churches, as well as individual Christians, must expect crucifixion when they are true to their Lord.) Much admired, however, is a collage sent to me by nuns from Oxfordshire, featuring the Virgin and Child. This includes a beautiful blue butterfly so life-like that visitors touch it, to make it fly away! Finally, some lines from T.S. Eliot's *Little Gidding* have been copied and placed in a large frame which formerly contained a not-very-inspiring holy picture.

If you came this way,
Taking any route, starting from anywhere,
At any time or at any season,
It would always be the same: you would have to put off
Sense and notion. You are not here to verify,
Instruct yourself, or inform curiosity
Or carry report. You are here to kneel
Where prayer has been valid. And prayer is more
Than an order of words, the conscious occupation
Of the praying mind, or the sound of the voice praying.
And what the dead had no speech for, when living,
They can tell you, being dead: the communication
Of the dead is tongued with fire beyond the language of the living.
Here, the intersection of the timeless moment
Is England and nowhere. Never and always.

And that's about it. A redundant medieval church, open daily for prayer . . . But within those walls I have been able to provide 'folk religion' for hundreds of people, 99 per cent of whom were not regular churchgoers. Here, people are never turned away because they are not good enough, or not members, or not regular attenders. Here, people are welcomed for their instinctive understanding of God in their ives – for their awareness that great events need special commemoration, that life is mysterious and beyond our control, that birth, and love, and death deserve to be marked worthily. 'Whosoever will may come.' To St Clement's they have come from my bus world, from the pub, from my other varied links with the life of the city – and from the fact that I have remained here for many years, recognised, known, and easily accessible:

'City Hall, please!'

'Sixty pence. Thank you!'

'Oh, it's you! My daughter has had another baby and we want you to christen it because you christened Martin and we all thought it was a lovely service. When can she come and see you?'

'I'll be in tonight, Next, please! Pass right down the car . . .'

For three reasons, I issue no service books at St Clement's. First, I possess none, other than some battered copies of *The Book of Common Prayer*, to which, as a Free Churchman, I could not dream of being bound, much as I love and raid it. Second, non-churchgoers make hard work of finding the relevant place in a book, and soon lose it again. The hunt to rediscover it prevents them concentrating on what is actually happening. In a similar way, the constant interjection of page and paragraph numbers by the minister (whilst sometimes necessary) easily becomes a distraction. It detracts from the momentum of the service, appears somehow amateurish, and erodes the sense of otherness. Third, the services I conduct, when required, at St Clement's do not appear together in any book. My basic document continues to be *The Book of Offices* of the Methodist Church, the service book with which I am most familiar but which, of course, has been replaced in recent years. To this I add the material I have culled from other sources. If it is good and will help to convey The Mystery, The Tenderness, and The Power to those who don't come to see us very often, I claim it for the gospel. We must be catholic and ecumenical in outlook, and no longer content to inherit the prejudices of ancient days. So there are no service books. The responsibility for making folk religion meaningful rests squarely upon the minister.

I have indicated, already, my attitude to infant baptism. For obvious pastoral reasons, I always try to direct parents to a church in their own neighbourhood whenever I receive enquiries about a christening. If they persist, however, I am quick to yield. All priests should be aware that insurmountable problems of communication are involved in the refusal to baptise a child. However reasonable the explanation, *the words simply do not register.* All that is conveyed is a sense of hurt and rejection which – because it is linked with something so precious and wonderful – engenders a resentment and hostility virtually guaranteed to last a lifetime. Happily, the reverse is also true. Welcome a little child in the sacrament of baptism, spend half an hour making its family realise that they are important and *special*, and you – and your church – will hold a special place in their affections for ever. I have found that infant baptisms are most effective performed singly; and – unless the parents are regular churchgoers – services separate from the church's normal Sunday worship cause less anxiety and embarrassment, and are much more appreciated.

I relish the opportunity infant baptism provides, to combine simple, meaningful folk religion with a clear and equally simple statement of the gospel. After welcoming family and friends to St Clement's 'on *Danielle*'s special day', I introduce the service by saying:

> Baptism is the rite of admission into the Christian church. The symbolism is simple and direct. We use water. Water is for cleansing. In baptism, it symbolises God washing away our sins. In the early church, baptisms were often held on Easter Day, and in the open air, using a river or the sea. Easter is the festival of dying and rising, and in this way the symbolism was strengthened. When the person was plunged beneath the water he was dying to his old way of life; when he came up, it was understood that he was rising to a new, Christian way of life. None of this applies exactly, of course, to an infant. *Danielle* has not yet had the time or the opportunity to develop the attitudes that we have developed: to sin as we have sinned. But she is a member of the human family, and corporately we all need God's acceptance and forgiveness and renewing power. Looked

at this way, infant baptism becomes a clear proclamation of the gospel, showing that God's love for us exists before we slide into that self-centredness which is sin, is unbroken by our sin, and continues for ever.

I then move straight on to the opening words of the service in *The Book of Offices*, which possess a dramatic quality that never fails:

Dearly Beloved, since it has pleased God to commit to human hands the care of this child, now brought here for holy baptism, let us recall both the promise and the warning of our Lord – the warning, how great is our offence if, by anything done or left undone, we put a stumbling-block in the way of one of His little ones; and the promise, that if we receive a little child in His Name, we receive the Lord Himself . . .

These are such *happy* occasions – and often attract large congregations of mainly non-churchgoers, who experience an environment of otherness and hear an announcement of the gospel – that I cannot understand the attitude of clergy prepared to turn such opportunities away.

The service always includes a clear statement of the duties of godparents:

The duty of godparents is to watch the growth and development of their godchildren – not in an interfering spirit, but with tenderness and affection. They stand in the wings as reserve parents. They should remember and pray for their godchildren, and endeavour to encourage a mature Christian commitment when their godchildren reach the age of understanding, and are able to confirm for themselves all that in baptism is done on their behalf. To that end, parents and godparents together make three vows: to provide a Christian home for the child; to order their own affairs in such a manner that the child suffers no avoidable or unnecessary hurt or handicap; to give the child access to the worship and teaching of the church.

The congregation move from their seats and gather round the font for the christening. The sanctifying of the water, the naming of the child, the pouring of the water and the signing with the Cross (together with the kiss, the showing of the child to the congregation – especially to the youngest members – the returning of the child to the mother, and any additional touches, like the presentation of some flowers), all combine to constitute surprisingly powerful drama, a theatre-in-the-round, with the audience pressed close and mingling with the players. Even the clicking of cameras doesn't seem out of place. These are memorable moments, to be enjoyed, captured, and recalled.

Then, back to the pews for the final prayers:

Almighty God, our heavenly Father, at this joyful family celebration we remember and give thanks to Thee for our own parents, and godparents, and all who were kind to us when we were small. May we not forget their goodness, but help us, when we can, to show our gratitude in acts of thoughtfulness and remembrance. Grant to those we loved who, now, are with Thee, eternal rest: may light perpetual shine upon them. We pray for the different homes represented here *this afternoon*. May our homes be places of peace and security and comfort and love and fun, with each member caring for the other, and all regarded as equally important and precious. May the example of Mary our Mother, who watched over the holy house at Nazareth, be our example and inspiration. We thank Thee for the happiness brought to our lives by children. Today, we pray especially for *Danielle*, whom we have brought to Thee in this holy sacrament and enrolled in the mystical fellowship of Thy holy church. May she grow in Thy love. May she have power over all the evil that is in the world, and be protected by Thy strength and grace. May everything good grow in her, until at last, she sees Thee in Thy glory; through Jesus Christ our Lord. Amen.

After the Lord's Prayer and the blessing, there follows the signing of the register, the presentation of the certificate, and more photographs and laughter in the churchyard. Religion has been dispensed, and the gospel proclaimed. Important things have been said, and new links of friendship have been forged. I cannot believe God disapproves.

Although the parish registers of St Clement date back to 1538, as a redundant church it is no longer licensed for weddings, and I am not an 'authorised person'. If people with whom I have come into touch through my ministry 'in the world' wish me to marry them, they have to follow what is, I believe, the custom in some continental countries. They must first appear before the registrar to undertake the civil and legal requirements; they can then come to church to repeat their vows before God in a setting of worship and celebration. Every church wedding combines these two elements – the civil and the religious – but it is perfectly possible to separate them.

As again I hinted earlier, weddings provide another glorious opportunity to offer a spiritual treat to people unfamiliar with worship. I enjoy weddings enormously. I agree, with D. H. Lawrence, that 'mankind has got to get back to the rhythm of the cosmos, and the permanence of marriage.' Yet I am also very tender and realistic towards divorcees, and try to help them whenever I can. I am not a tame priest who – on this or any other matter – can be easily manipulated; the few who have tried have quickly been corrected. Each application for a re-marriage in church I consider very carefully, *and sometimes decline*; but I also bear in mind that the gospel is about the eternal possibility of making new beginnings. I am not interested in the practice of refusing a wedding but offering a 'blessing'. That strikes me as a grudging and cowardly kind of compromise which satisfies nobody, and means very little. It is like saying: 'We wash our hands of this matter – but wish you all the best!' Marriage for life is the gospel ideal. Yet human nature is frail, relationships end, love dies. But when new relationships are born and love flourishes again, the gospel message of new birth, new hope and new life encourages me to offer a second chance in the name of Christ. Great moments of idealism should be welcomed, and seized upon with enthusiasm and professionalism. Remarriages enable us to provide folk religion with a high gospel content, including expressions of penitence, forgiveness and thanksgiving.

I always tell couples whom I marry in St Clement's that they must regard the *two* appointments kept in the previous hour – with the registrar and with me – as the two halves which, together, form their wedding. I concede that the legal side is important. I assert that the religious side is equally important:

> The uniting of two lives has tremendous implications, for the rest of the community as well as for the people concerned. It is not just a question of signing a piece of paper. At such crucial moments in life, men and women have always turned to religion, because religion lifts the imagination, and gives us vision and hope, and inspires us, and makes us *want* to be good and true. That is why I am glad you wanted to come to church today. It is the right place to begin, properly, your new, married life together. I love this old church where, over the

centuries, hundreds of couples have stood where you are standing now. I hope that, from today, you will love it, too, and will remember this great occasion whenever you pass St Clement's . . .

At weddings, I usually pursue the Lawrencian, and utterly Christian, theme of the permanence of marriage being linked to the round of the seasons and the passage of time. A man is different at twenty, thirty, forty, fifty, sixty, seventy, and the woman at his side is different, too. As summer follows winter and year follows year, they are the same, yet different; and in the interplay, the conjunction, the balance and the relationship between these changes, the music of the marriage is produced, and the various movements of the symphony gradually constructed. These things are true, and all worth stating (and people *listen*). For those reasons, requests for marriage (and, often, re-marriage) should be grasped eagerly, examined, and granted whenever possible – not dismissed with a glance down the nose because the people seeking our services are not regular worshippers, and therefore may be deemed to be 'using' us. We cannot afford to reject people if we genuinely wish to witness to the Divine Love, and contribute to the life of the nation. In any case, *we are there to be used* – like our Lord.

One bride had set her heart on having church bells at her wedding, but the three bells at St Clement's had been wedged because their medieval frames were rotten, and they could not be swung in safety. With the aid of three clothes-lines and some pieces of smooth, heavy scrap metal from the bus garage, I devised a Heath Robinson arrangement which enabled a youth who had ascended the tower staircase to ring the bells with impressive effect. In the churchyard, I found myself almost in tears as I heard the joyful sound! It seemed to express and celebrate the catholicism, the versatility, the humanity, the determination, the commitment, and the love for the 'outsider' for which St Clement's stood.

Funerals and memorial services bring to our churches people who are distressed and vulnerable. For them – with great tenderness – we have to create an atmosphere which permits the expression of grief, but also contains words of hope and healing. It is a solemn responsibility, and, in times of particular tragedy, can be daunting and harrowing. Here, above all, sensitivity and skill are demanded; yet, once more, these services present us with some of our most precious opportunities to minister effectively to the hearts and minds of people from beyond the gap.

Not long ago, I conducted the funeral of a retired charge hand from the garage. The service was well attended, and I used my normal, straightforward selection of sentences, readings, and prayers. In a brief address, I spoke openly of the deceased's complete lack of religious faith, but recalled that he was an exceptionally gifted engineer. I observed that life was a mystery to which we all responded individually. Where *I* tried to interpret it with hymns and Bibles and prayers, Gilbert had interpreted it with craftsmanship and a spanner. We were all made differently; a tool-box meant no more to me than a prayer-book did to Gilbert! Athough these were complicated matters, I suggested that we had both been engaged in something basic and fundamental to human life; we had both been trying to interpret and understand the universe as we experienced it; we had both – in our own ways – been searching for the order, the cause, the explanation, the reason, and the meaning that lay behind every facet of this physical existence. In my religious language, we had both been responding to God, and searching for God – Gilbert, with his sleeves rolled up; me, with my hands together!

I had not intended to say any of this. I was making it up

as I went along. But suddenly, I became aware that everyone present was hanging on every word. You could have heard a pin drop. Gilbert with a halo was hard to imagine; but Gilbert's mechanical skills presented as a valid response to the God of truth was a new and arresting thought. So I pushed it further.

All the neighbours had turned to Gilbert whenever their cars had needed attention. The road in front of his house was an open-air workshop, and a glimpse of his feet protruding from beneath the car on which he was working was often the only clue to his whereabouts. Here was more evidence of religion – and *real* religion at that. The skills Gilbert had acquired and the insight he had been given were not kept, meanly, to himself, but were shared generously with all who needed help – just as Jesus taught us . . . You see? You don't *have* to sing hymns . . . Religion is also about truth and understanding, and kindness and sharing . . .

After the service, a man who had worked with Gilbert for many years spoke one strange sentence which I shall always remember. Clearly moved, he gripped my hand, and in his blunt, country manner said: 'That was *good*, that was' . . . And we all felt the same. The service had *worked*. Yet, only days later, I met a former busman who was uncharacteristically close to tears as he told me of the funeral of his friend, who had died recently in a road accident. The tears were not simply those of grief, but of disappointment and frustration that the funeral seemed to have no meaningful connection with his friend. It didn't capture and channel the emotions everyone was experiencing, nor 'round things off', but left the mourners feeling there was unfinished business to attend to, and more things still to be said . . . That is a reaction I have encountered many times over the years. Funerals – unlike weddings and christenings – have to be pitched at different levels, according to the circumstances, and call for the highest standards of compassion and professional competence. The marriage of dignity and warmth is indispensable here as nowhere else. I have an outline which provides the framework for my funeral addresses, and which I adjust, as required; but the basic ingredients remain the same.

Frequently, I begin by observing that the pitiful inadequacy of speech is a fact with which we are all familiar, but it is brought home to us never more powerfully than on such occasions. To frame any words at all seems a tremendous and futile effort – yet there is so much we want to communicate.

We want to express our sympathy, our love, and our grief to the bereaved family. On particularly tragic occasions, we find ourselves wanting to express something which at first glance might be described as anger, but which keeps dissolving in helplessness and bewilderment, leaving us numb and empty. We want to say things about the faith of the church: the hope that – in Mother Julian's words – 'All shall be well, and all shall be well, and all manner of thing shall be well.' Above all, we want to say things about the departed as we knew her/him as mother/father, wife/husband, daughter/son, friend, neighbour, workmate . . .

Those [I might continue] are some of the reasons we have crowded into this ancient holy place. It doesn't matter if our thoughts are confused, if our words die on our lips, or even if our sadness overflows. Our Blessed Lord wept at the death of his friend Lazarus. The important thing is that *we have come* – from family, from work . . . to offer the only gifts which lie, now, within our power to offer: our presence, and our attention.

We form, like any congregation, a varied assortment; but in this moment we are united by the departed [whom I will call Helen, to commemorate a brave and gifted woman whose funeral I conducted in a tiny village church, on a sunny afternoon long ago]. We are united by *Helen*; in this moment, our differences are transcended; *together*, we are commemorating a person. By our attention we are seeking to express the meaning of a life. That is the ultimate significance of this occasion. And in so doing, we are also making statements about the meaning of our own lives. Our common humanity means that we are involved in *Helen*'s life and death and their significance, and involved in this service.

We hold her in our hearts and minds today with tenderness and affection, recalling all that she meant to us, and will continue to mean . . .

Words of reminiscence, recollection, and tribute follow. These, obviously, are more effective when the minister has known the departed. There is no need to paint a full warts-and-all portrait: emphasising the positive and the good will suffice. But a gently humorous memory or observation is invariably welcome, and the combined tears and smiles help to provide an essential release. It is at this point in the address I include reflections like those made at Gilbert's funeral.

Usually, I conclude with thoughts along the following lines:

Our lives and our universe find their ultimate meaning in the mystery and greatness of God. The permanence of this physical world is an illusion; everything is changing, everything is in a state of flux. The most minute detail of this shimmering, moving creation is a revelation of God: every leaf, every human situation, every face. Today we commemorate and celebrate *Helen*. We do so in the knowledge that *Helen*'s learning and courage and understanding and service are part of the

eternal meaning and purpose of Jesus Christ, and therefore shall continue and multiply throughout all ages, for
ever held in the hands of God.

We have shared life with *Helen*, and come now to
stand with her. Jesus asked His disciples to watch with
Him in the Garden when the time of His passion and
death drew near. We would stand with *our* friends – in
their life, at their death, and as they journey through
worlds unknown. In our prayers and hymns today, *that
is what we are doing*: standing before God, wearing a
common humanity, standing *with Helen* and *for Helen*.
And if our eyes swim and our words fail, *it doesn't matter*. For all that we *could* say, or *would* say, in our deepest
and most loving moments, is being said for us *now* – is
being said for us eternally – by Jesus Christ as He offers
Himself, our Great High Priest. 'Thou that hearest the
prayer', said the psalmist, 'unto Thee shall all flesh
come.'

Funerals of people who have been active members of
the church have a dimension which is lacking, inevitably,
in folk religion funerals. Yet the latter, too, can be memorable. The grief of the bereaved must be our first consideration; but the notes of celebration and thanksgiving must
also be stressed. So much hangs upon the temperament
and sensitivity of the minister. If a shaft of sunlight suddenly pierces the church, or a crash of thunder fills the
mourners with awe, or a blackbird sings loudly on a
branch outside the window, or the sunshine of a spring
morning or an autumn afternoon is so beautiful it hurts,
we should be quick to acknowledge it, draw it into what
we are doing, and make a metaphor or parable from it.
Such alertness is well rewarded. I am sure that the people
who regard me most warmly are those for whom I once
conducted the funeral of a loved one.

However, it was the funeral of Arthur which I will always associate with the provison of folk religion at its most effective. Arthur was a bus driver who had visited Djakarta and had married Lina there, two years previously. Their wedding pictures looked like stills from *South Pacific*. Alas, the fairy-tale was short-lived. Arthur became ill, and bone cancer was diagnosed. I visited him at home and in hospital, on one occasion leaving the bus at the hospital gates while I spent a few moments with him. Arthur was no churchgoer, but as everything he treasured began to slip away, he found – like many before him – that the traditional words of the church began to sound slightly more real, and in the promises of the gospel he found faith enough to face the end with courage and calm.

Lina's mother arrived, too late to comfort Arthur but in time to support her daughter. I looked at her in awe: so small, oriental, and grief-stricken, but with a resolve which had brought her alone, with no word of English, from the far side of the globe. At airports and railway stations she had stood helplessly with a card bearing her name hung around her neck, and one of a series of others held in front, pre-prepared and bearing requests like, 'Please Mr Driver take this lady to station for Norwich train.'

Christianity is not the largest religion in Indonesia, a land where many faiths and religious traditions meet, but Lina was a Christian. On the night before the funeral, I conducted a ceremony at the closing of the coffin. I had asked Lina what rituals would have been observed at home, and simplified the answers I received. In Djakarta, all Lina's friends and relations would have been present. Here, at the tiny chapel of rest, I stood at one side of the open coffin, the two weeping women stood at the other side, and the undertaker waited in the doorway. Arthur was wearing his wedding suit. I watched for ten minutes as the women pinned about forty carnations around the inside of the coffin, at the top, forming a border. The effect was striking and very touching. A nod indicated that all was ready. I read a short lesson, spoke simply about it for two minutes, took a deep breath and sang – quietly and unaccompanied – the Russian *Kontakion* (which I felt, in the circumstances, would convey more than any attempt to stagger through 'Abide with me'), and closed with prayers. A bottle of scent was produced, and the widow shook scent liberally over the body; the bottle passed, in turn, to her mother, myself, and the undertaker. As I solemnly sprinkled him, a picture of Arthur sitting in the canteen at work flashed into my mind. With the chapel filled with fragrance, the lid of the coffin was closed.

With all her wedding guests many miles away, Lina wanted some photographs of the funeral to send home to her family. A bus driver accepted this difficult assignment. The undertaker had suggested a service in the cemetery chapel; with kindly firmness, I turned this idea aside. Fancy coming from a land rich in ceremony and colour to sit in a cemetery chapel! I explained that St Clement's would have incomparably more atmosphere, and they would carry away memories to cherish. Instinctively, they understood and were grateful.

If photographs were required, I decided that the processional cross was essential – but I could find nobody to carry it. In desperation, I asked my bus conductor. Not surprisingly, he demurred! I told him he was young enough, fit enough, and handsome enough, and that, in any case, it was his *duty* to do it, for Arthur. Finally, he bravely consented. He, too, wasn't a churchgoer, but I did not consider that a disqualification. The cross *had* to be carried; there was a job to be done. God's love embraces us all; and personal considerations were not relevant; willingness to serve was the one thing needful. So – just as we operated our bus together – we did this job together; for Arthur.

Tony was superb. Following instructions, he walked slowly and held the cross high – as if he'd been doing it all his life. I have found, time and again, that young people are natural catholics. If you can get them into a cassock and give them a cross or a candle to carry, they will usually perform with style, flair, and enjoyment. How much they have lost by forfeiting the churchgoing habit! An entire dimension of human experience, and a vehicle for conveying the most vital sentiments of all, have gone.

I switched on the antiquated church heating twelve hours prior to the service, terrified that the old woman might take a chill. An hour before we began, I burned incense to symbolise our prayers and contribute to a sense of otherness. A photograph of Arthur, with candles each side and a bowl of Christmas roses from my garden in front, stood on a table near the door. Many busmen, with the depot superintendent, were present.

Tony and I met the cortège at the gate. My purple stole signified our sadness. As we moved towards the church I read verses from Psalm 51, switching to the familiar Sentences as we entered. Tony stood beside me throughout – one step to the right, and one step back. It proved a powerful and unforgettable occasion. Nobody could fail to be moved by the grieving, foreign women. Conscious of old Mrs Kurniawan's inability to understand the language, I had – with Lina's help – prepared a few words in Indonesian. Written phonetically, they still looked forbidding and I was tempted to shirk them: but that would have been an admission of failure. *Without explanation*, I concluded the address by saying: '*Hari inni karmi; sarlammat tingal Arthur; isti rahat dernyan Tuhan; karmi selalu arkan mungingat mo.*' A profound, potent stillness filled the church.

I sprinkled the coffin with holy water as a sign of the divine cleansing, using an evergreen twig from the churchyard and walking unhurriedly round the coffin, making the Sign of the Cross as the water was applied. Then followed the commendation:

> Arthur, May the Blood of our Saviour cleanse thee from every stain of sin, refresh thee and give thee eternal life; May Angels lead thee to Paradise; May the Martyrs welcome thee as thou drawest near to the Heavenly City; May Mary our Mother protect thee and comfort us who mourn.

Tony led us slowly from the church – and was horrified that I expected him to ride in the hearse to the cemetery! There, he led us to the grave – with virtually the entire congregation following, anxious to miss nothing. Coming from the far side of the gap, it occurred to nobody to ask which form of service I had been following. Intuitively, they apprehended that – at a time of tragedy and deep sadness – they had been able, by their presence and attention, to express their thoughts and emotions in ritual both worthy and satisfying. The terrible thing had been lanced. The healing could begin.

The steward at the service was a local Methodist, Archie Fraser, who watched the service with a shrewd Scottish eye and recognised its strength and authenticity. It was dramatic yet simple. Every word and gesture was meaningful and intelligible, yet the sense of worship and mystery was retained. We felt that something real had taken place. It was catholic Christianity with a Methodist heart – the kind of effective blend at which we would, by now, have become adept if earlier proposals for church unity had not been timorously rejected. Everyone present seemed affected, and the crowning tribute came later in the day when I called at the house. The old woman spoke to her daughter, and Lina translated: 'Mami says "It was just like being at home".'

Many people still value an opportunity at the graveside, to throw earth on the coffin. It is a simple and respectful tribute: a small act of personal involvement in the ritual, providing a moment of contact and vital connection. It is a recognition of our common, frail humanity, and an expression of love. The person sprinkling the earth is saying: 'Soon, I will be as you are now; in the meantime, I mingle my dust with yours – in memory, in gratitude, and in love.' 'For dust thou art, and unto dust shalt thou return.'

Not all non-churchgoers are highly intelligent. The worship most likely to make an impact upon them must be something felt and seen, rather than something to be thought about. Yet they respond to excellence in worship, and will listen attentively to a short, well-sung anthem. I believe that the mixture of ingredients we employ at St Clement's has achieved a surprising consensus of approval. Our traditions *can* be made to blend – to the benefit of us all.

Sometimes, folk religion has to be provided off church premises. At St Clement's, for example, Christmas is celebrated on a home-and-away basis. On the Sunday before Christmas I conduct an evening of lusty carol singing in a local tavern, perched on a window ledge or on the top of a step-ladder. This is a lively, no-holds-barred, stand-up-and-sock-it-to-them occasion which has become very popular over the years. It is always referred to, touchingly, as 'the carol service', but it is a night of community singing, banter and much fun. Exausted, hoarse, and with my cassock soaked in sweat, I close the evening with a short prayer and a blessing. For many people, it has come to mark the begining of the Christmas season.

I see many of the same faces at the return fixture, which is the midnight mass by candlelight at St Clement's on Christmas Eve. The redundant church, with no members, slowly fills with people from across the gap – busworkers, revellers, friends from the pub – all longing, on this special night, for a hint of the presence of God with us. The old church never disappoints them. Ten years after he first squeezed into a tiny cassock at the age of eight, the land-lord's son arrived breathless at the church, straight from work, just in time to carry a processional candle in what is normally his only church service of the year. God has not used me to convert many people; but how is it possible to evaluate that kind of loyalty and enthusiasm? Folk religion makes people's lives fuller, deeper, and richer, and makes the world a sweeter place.

If some are shocked at what they see as a nonconformist occasionally playing unauthorised high-church games, they have missed the point. They have overlooked my commit-ment to bridging the gap, and my determination to use every legitimate means at my disposal to achieve that end. My pastoral ministry, since the late 1960s, has been directed almost entirely towards the needs of non-churchgoers, but this chapter has been written in no spirit of arrogance. I know it describes nothing which is not being done ten times better in hundreds of parish churches, and says nothing which is not being said more clearly by others. Neither have I foolishly attempted to imply that only ritu-alistic forms of worship minister effectively to non-churchgoers. I have not done so because it is not true. Dignity, warmth, sensitivity and imagination are what is required – though gesture, symbol, and colour *are* import-ant. I have merely reflected on the unusual opportunity which fell to me to provide, over many years, a sanctuary of holiness and tranquillity, and to supply various forms of religion-on-demand, which I call folk religion. I have made no great claims, and I have drawn no weighty conclusions. However, on one point there should be no confusion. If we believe, as I do, that all God's children have the right to worship their Heavenly Father, they also have the right to expect the help of His servants in the preparation and presentation of that worship. Their requests should be welcomed and dealt with seriously and generously, unless we are content to see ourselves as members of an exclusive, favoured *sect* – which is a far cry from the grand, all-embracing, Trinitarian faith of the Holy Catholic Church.

Occasionally, people make unusual requests. I have been asked to conduct funerals with the religious content kept to an absolute minimum, out of respect to the views of the deceased. Such honesty and sensitivity are commendable – though no Christian minister would wish to travel far down that particular path. Other considerations apart, funerals – like weddings – involve more than the immediate small circle of participants. The needs of the wider congregation have also to be kept in mind. Discussion and mutual respect, however, will normally produce an honourable compromise. One of the most powerful funerals I was ever privileged to conduct – that of a greatly respected trade unionist and socialist – was planned against a background of just such negotiation.

Other requests are truly inspired. At a wedding I attended as a guest, the young bridegroom asked for a Stevie Wonder song, 'Isn't She Lovely?' to be played by the organist as a voluntary during the signing of the register. She was! – and the item created a moving effect which moistened the eyes of many in the congregation, including one particularly hardened observer of the ecclesiastical scene!

In *The Life of Hugh Price Hughes*, written by his daughter, there is a reference to the old parish church of St Peter, Carmarthen:

> The old church, consecrated by the great life events of the townspeople, and sheltering within itself the shattered flags of great British wars, must have made a life-long impression on their children, to which my father

was the last to be insensible. Once, at assize time, when the judge and corporation came in state to the old church and streamed up the aisle with the sunlight glancing on the scarlet and ermine from the high, narrow windows, he whispered smilingly to the friend of his youth, a staunch Anglican, 'You beat us in this, Tom.' Then – for it was after he had begun to take an interest in religious matters – 'I can quite understand your reverence for this old church, and am rather envious that we have not a Methodist chapel of the same age and association.' His eyes flashing over the scene sufficiently indicated what the 'this' signified. It was that tradition, that veneration for the past, which he was to appear to combat and to which, in the imagination of some, he seemed to be insensible. There was never a greater error.

When first I read that lovely pasage, thirty years ago, I little dreamed that one day I would stream up a cathedral nave in state, accompanying the visiting High Court judge! More surprisingly, still, is the fact that I had cause to process, in civic robes, up the aisle *of that very church*, for during my shrievalty, the national association of sheriffs held its annual meeting at Carmarthen, and Divine service was held in St Peter's!

Occasions of that nature raise another aspect of the provision of folk religion: the complex issue of church and state. I am not among those who rue the day the Emperor Constantine made Christianity the official religion of the Roman Empire. I can see all the snags: the lure of power, wealth, and preferment; the temptations and the corruptions; the nullifying and prostituting of the gospel for temporal, materialistic, or nationalistic ends. But I can also see the dream of a Christianised society, and, despite the anomalies, I value positive links between church and state. They help to prevent the church from becoming marginalised, and give it exceptional opportunities to witness and serve. A genuine establishment would be daring, unconventional,. and breathtakingly beautiful. If society said. 'We wish our laws and our common life to express the principles of the Kingdom: hold us to that vision, and help us to pursue it and make it come true!' – we would, indeed, feel that the New Jerusalem was at hand. If church leaders lived in near-poverty, society would be perpetually challenged by such a standing rebuke to accepted standards. Sadly, the reality is less exciting. Nevertheless, I am glad to see bishops in the second chamber of Parliament, judges attending Divine service, and the sovereign crowded in an act of Christian worship and dedication. I write, however, as a Free Churchman; I have no right to comment on Anglicanism, or to discuss whether the price paid for establishment is too high. And in a multi-faith society, the nature of establishment may alter drastically in years to come. If our discipleship was more costly and more convincing, our impact would be very much greater on all those occasions when society requires religious ministrations. It isn't always easy to walk the tight-rope between dynamic and prophetic Christian discipleship and apparent support for the existing order of society, but it is possible if we keep our gaze concentrated upon the Love of Jesus. We have to live in the society in which God has placed us – particularly if we want to change it.

Christianity is still, for the moment, the accepted official religion in our land, and for all the inherent incongruity of the situation, we should be grateful. We should seize the opportunities to point to Jesus, and stop worrying about preserving the unsullied purity of our religion. A great deal that we take for granted in our society stems from the fact that Christianity has, for centuries, been the religion of the nation. Our schools and hospitals, and some of the worthiest traits in our national character (like the traditional British sense of fair play) owe much to their Christian origins.

A classic example of the tensions possible when society's urgent request for folk religion jars the Christian conscience is seen each year on Remembrance Sunday. The dangers of appearing to glorify war, or of depicting God as British, are self-evident. Yet there are many positive things concerning peace, justice, service to the community, forgiveness, reconciliation, comradeship, courage and self-sacrifice which we ought to be able to say. And we ought to have things to say about life and death to people who are remembering dear ones they have loved and lost. If *we* cannot, who can? (Incidentally, what a pity that the powerful and evocative tune, 'Supreme Sacrifice', is fading into disuse because the words of 'O valiant hearts' are deemed unsuitable. The tune is too valuable to lose.)

It was in Antioch that the followers of Jesus were first dubbed 'Christians'. They certainly didn't win the title because they went to church to get married, or called in a priest when somebody died, or sang a hymn at their cup final. The name was given because they preached Christ, centred their lives upon Him, and continued steadfastly in the apostles' doctrine, and fellowship, and the breaking of bread, and the prayers. 'If only things could have stayed like that . . .' Such a silly and unworthy thought is rather like wishing we could have remained little children for ever.

It was inevitable that, sooner or later, Christians would have to decide whether to cast off, accept opportunities and responsibilities, and try to implement the message of Love as widely as possible in God's world – or opt for the spiritual kindergarten and remain 'untainted' by the world, in cosy isolation. With all its difficulties and compromises, the right course was obvious. It is obvious still. In recent years, as the longing for a renewal of Christian faith and experience has intensified, our criticism of formal, nominal discipleship has sharpened. (I have been critical in this book.) When this has the effect of encouraging Christians to a greater commitment and an eagerness to fathom the depths of their religion, that is good. But when it leads us to underestimate the importance of 'official religion', to turn away children, and to despise the 'shallow' religion of the majority, it is not good. All religious occasions have missionary potential: all witness to the Love of God, and all are capable of increasing the spiritual experience of the participants by extending – be it ever so slightly – the frontiers of awareness. I have returned to that demanding, dual responsibility laid upon us: to urge men and women to explore all the unsearchable riches of Christ; and to provide, with quiet authority, authentic religious rites for a community uncertain what, if anything, it believes.

'So You Must Follow Me'

Geoffrey Anketell Studdert-Kennedy – devoted priest and chaplain to the forces in the First World War, best known by his army nickname of 'Woodbine Willie' – knew a thing or two about crossing the gap and speaking to all types of people in plain language. His dialect poem, 'Well?' which begins:

> Our padre were a solemn bloke,
>   We called 'im dismal Jim . . .'

is a devotional classic. In it, a cockney Tommy, in reflective mood, tells of an unforgettable dream in which he caught a glimpse of God:

> It seemed to me as though 'Is face
>   Were millions rolled in one;
> It never changed yet always changed,
>   Like the sea beneath the sun.
> 'Twere all men's face yet no man's face
>   And a face no man can see,
> And it seemed to say in silent speech,
>   'Ye did 'em all to Me.
> The dirty things ye did to 'em,
>   The filth ye thought was fine,
> Ye did 'em all to Me', it said,
>   'For all their souls were Mine.'
> All eyes were in 'Is eyes – all eyes,
>   My wife's and a million more;
> And once I thought as those two eyes
>   Were the eyes of the London whore.
> And they was sad – my Gawd, 'ow sad,
>   Wiv tears what seemed to shine,
> And quivering bright wi' the speech o' light
>   They said, ''Er soul was Mine.'

And then at last 'E said one word,
  'E just said one word – 'Well?'
And I said in a funny voice,
  'Please can I go to 'Ell?'

That last line has stuck in my mind. In a curious way, it captures the feel of everything I have said in this book. Why would anyone ask to go to hell? For love! When our hearts have been overwhelmed by the Love of Jesus, we shall be willing to face the 'hell' of prolonged exposure to human sin and suffering, by deliberately engaging in costly, long-term forms of evangelism in the world. When our vision has been fired by the Love of Jesus, we shall be willing to endure the 'hell' of open political commitment on behalf of the vulnerable and the poor, and the hatred and misunderstanding likely to flow from it.

I have not tried to pretend it is easy to get back in touch with ordinary people. It is not. It takes an effort to climb out of our Christian sub-culture – with its comforting songs, in-language, and fellowship – to become strangers and aliens among the unbelievers. It requires courage to *remain* there, waiting for the moment, earning the right to be heard.

Gradually, as we learn the ropes, it becomes easier – yet, in other ways, mission becomes more and more demanding the longer we remain 'in the world'. Increasingly, I find that keeping a high profile over many years – being constantly visible and immediately recognised – becomes a considerable drain upon nervous energy and spiritual resources. There is no let-up – and only the smallest possible margin for mistakes. 'The wilderness and the solitary place', together with the stillness of ancient holy sites, are now – for me –indispensable.

'Please can I go to hell?' Jesus looks at us quizzically, to see if we mean it. Then He answers: 'Yes! And I will come

with you! – I will never leave thee, nor forsake thee.' And
He is better than His word. He goes on ahead! Cross over
the bridge and you will find that Jesus is already there, in
his world, wondering what has delayed you. 'If I make my
bed in hell, behold thou art there.'

But, in the poem, it is shame which prompts the plea:
'Please can I go to hell?' Shame is the only possible response when the immensity of the Divine Love dawns upon
us. It is the response of Isaiah in the temple: 'Woe is me! for
I am undone; because I am a man of unclean lips . . . for
mine eyes have seen the King . . .' It is the response of
Simon Peter: 'Depart from me; for I am a sinful man.' It is
the reason I shrink from any hint of undue familiarity in
Christian thought and worship. The nearer we draw to
God, the more uncomfortable we become; the self-
knowledge which His love imparts is devastating and unbearable. We are saved only by God's unutterable tenderness. These are the chords our doctrine and our worship
must strike if we are to awaken an echoing response in the
hearts and minds of the unconvinced and the unconverted.
The God of whom we speak is not neat and manageable,
but immense and terrible. His Love is not sugary; it is
searing, and causes us to mumble: 'Please can I go to hell?'

But this time, God refuses. He loves us; and He wants
us; and He wants our service:

> And 'E stood there and looked at me,
>   And 'E kind o' seemed to grow,
> Til 'E shone like the sun above my 'ed,
>   And then 'E answered 'No.
> You can't, that 'Ell is for the blind,
>   And not for those that see.
> You know that you 'ave earned it, lad,
>   So you must follow Me . . .'

Christianity is not a vocation, nor a hobby, but a way of
life. It is about following Jesus. You can do lots of religious

things, and not be following Jesus. You can appreciate nature, enjoy philosophical debate, or revel in the glories of English church music, *and still miss Jesus*. That's why our witness doesn't ring true. Too many of us mouth the words but are a million miles away from *the experience* – the experience of being shamed, thrilled, and overwhelmed by the love of Jesus.

From the details contained in the Gospels, we all construct pictures of what we imagine Jesus was like. Among non-churchgoers, these range from the vague and the infantile to the bizarre and the wistful. Much more imaginative and interesting are portraits like Dennis Potter's *Son of Man*, though I find his tormented, self-doubting Jesus moving but ultimately unconvincing. I have always been particularly grateful for the picture of Jesus presented by Lloyd Douglas in *The Robe* and *The Big Fisherman*. His Jesus is close to the one who steps from the pages of the New Testament to confront me, and to bid me follow Him.

People listened when Jesus spoke; all kinds of people – and the children, too, for whom He always had time. His presence had an extraordinary effect. He could make people feel ashamed, or confident, or thankful, or brave, without uttering a word. His eyes must have been indescribable. Ask Peter! They could rebuke, question, reassure, or forgive. You couldn't pretend to Jesus, because He seemed to know, already. There was laughter and fun when He was about, and those eyes sparkled; yet, sometimes, they were filled with a deep and terrible sadness, which mystified and troubled his closest friends. All who carried a burden of any kind suddenly realised it had lifted, after they had been with Jesus. The sick and the poor and the outcasts trailed after Him, and He never turned them away. He taught that we should love one another: that was the way to be free. And he talked a lot about a Kingdom . . .

One of the loveliest encounters described in the New Testament is the meeting between Jesus and the woman of Samaria beside the well at Sychar. After a few rounds of verbal sparring, Jesus came to the point and, seizing the metaphor of the moment, He offered her 'living water'. Seconds later, pointing to the well, he added: 'Whosoever drinketh of this water shall thirst again: but whosoever drinketh of the water that I shall give him shall never thirst; but the water that I shall give him shall be in him a well of water springing up into everlasting life.'

Jesus was saying: 'Relax; stop worrying; stop wasting your life with trivial and sordid little concerns; stop kidding yourself that the universe revolves around *you*; stop grasping and grabbing. Try a new way. Try gentleness; try kindness; try patience; try compassion; try forgiveness – try singing! And see what happens! See how other people will improve! See what peace and happiness you will find in your own heart. See what a burden will be lifted. See how free you will become!'

What He said to her, He says to us. He offers *us* a vision of His love. He sketches a picture of His Kingdom, and He says, 'Follow me.' And until we have seen the beauty and simplicity of it all, and have begun to follow Jesus ourselves, we shall not persuade others to drink from the well of Living Water. Most ministers are based in the church, and make missionary 'raids' on the world; I am based in the world, and make raids upon the church. There is a raid on now! Looking in from outside, I am saddened by the gap, and exasperated by the tepid discipleship with which we hope to span it. Our Faith is so *harmless*! We are seldom seen as a threat, because nothing fills us with passion and indignation. We were given a beautiful globe to inhabit and we've abused it; in our own country, houses, factories and roads are covering more and more of the open countryside, and quiet places are becoming hard to find. We should be filled with indignation and alarm. Cars seem to multiply every year, destroying our towns and polluting the atmosphere. Public transport – which enables the young, the old, the poor, and non-drivers to enjoy and explore the creation – seems under constant threat. We take these kinds of things in our stride; indeed, it hardly occurs to us that there might be a connection between them and the gospel. Sometimes we excuse our inaction by thinking: 'The problems are too large; what *I* do will make no difference.' That is not a Christian judgement; to live as if it *would* make a difference is to acquire stature. Again, Christians are, rightly, concerned about issues of law and order – but we should never wash our hands of *any* person, and should also be known as the friends of publicans and sinners; but we are so respectable and so conformist that our paths never cross. *Where is the audacity in our faith?* Where is the outrageous confidence that Jesus has set us free and made us brothers and sisters, and given us the world to share? Why do we join everyone else in craving for more, and bigger, and better, when we already have sufficient? Where is our contentment? Why have we declined the freedom Jesus offers? The flowers in your garden are for me to enjoy, too – once I am free from envy, jealousy, and possessiveness. 'Ye will not come to me, that ye might have life . . . But I know you, that ye have not the love of God in you.'

The impact of our witness to those who have no faith increases in direct proportion to the depth of our commitment to Jesus and His teaching. It becomes *most* potent when it is also linked to that dimension of otherness to which I have referred constantly. Christianity is not *only* about seeking a just society, and not *only* about being serene and forgiving in personal relationships. Christian discipleship should include a heightened awareness of the tremendous mystery which lies beneath the surface of human existence and, not infreqently, breaks through:

Silent am I now and still,
Dare not in Thy presence move.

At the east end of St Clement's, the highway is very
narrow. Often, I stand in the street between the church
and the old houses opposite, and think of the people and
objects which have passed through that confined space:
carriers' carts; pilgrims; open-topped tramcars; mediaeval
mayors and aldermen on horseback . . . That, alone, is a
fascinating mental exercise. But then I go into the church,
and I stand before the altar. Maybe I light the candles, and
they flicker in the draught, in the darkness. And as I stare,
one part of my mind knows exactly what lies beyond the
drapery and the ancient east wall – a narrow street, cur-
rently adorned with all the trappings of human life in the
1990s. To another part of my mind, however, those facts
are irrelevant and almost unreal. The deep stillness, the
candles, the symbolism of cross and altar, the over-
arching, all-pervading biblical tradition which provides the
packaging to make vast concepts manageable, the sense of
history mingling with a sense of timelessness, the slightly
awesome feeling of holiness – these all combine to tell me
something which seems more true, and much more meaningful: that behind the altar, on the other side of that wall,
stretches eternity.

That is the kind of experience which makes old
churches so interesting and valuable. You can, of course,
be sensitive to such moments and not follow Jesus; but
you cannot commit yourself to the Way of Love and be
unmindful of The Mystery. There is an eternal dimension
to Christian discipleship which adds authority to our witness and makes following Jesus a continuous and unfolding adventure. Those who find joy and fulfilment in the
Christian life long for others to discover it, too. More of
us, therefore, must examine the quality of our discipleship
– then ask to go to hell! We have a message and an experi-

ence to share. People are so hungry for love that, when they get to know you, they will drain you dry. But they will never hear if we remain in church, too scared to get up and out; too timid to cross the gap.

Whatever you understand by 'God', *God is Love* – that is our message. We are not here to get richer and richer, or to discover everything, or even to cultivate a narrow concern for our own personal salvation. We are here to love one another, as Jesus taught us, and to love the world in which He has placed us. God loves us all – the small number who attend church, the much greater number who seldom come near. Those of us who hear the gospel week by week must ask ourselves, repeatedly, whether our familiarity with the message has blunted its cutting edge, and dulled our commitment. '*Love one another.*' It has inescapable political implications of the most radical nature. It has personal implications, equally searching and demanding. And it has cosmic and eternal dimensions which, for the most part, we apprehend only through a glass, darkly: through the wonder of the universe; through the body of a lover; through a song or a laugh or a sigh; through inspired Scriptures; through a mystic rite: through bread and wine. Unity in Diversity, and Diversity in Unity. The One, Loving God is active throughout.

But God *everywhere* can become God *nowhere*; God in *all things* can lead to God in *nothing*: specific times and places are important. *Worship* is the mortar which binds together our doctrines, our personal discipleship, and our social vision. It should be the chief source of our spiritual nourishment, providing an ethereal counterpoint to daily involvement in the life of world. In addition, it still supplies many of our best missionary opportunities (which is why I have discussed it at such length). In worship, we attempt to express our response to The Mystery, our commitment to the Way of Love, and our longing for new energy and power. It should be an essentially joyous activity, where awe and reverence blend with warmth and acceptance; where we are 'touched with loving sympathy'; and where 'silence heightens heaven'.

But when the worship ends, we have to return again to our task. Serious discipleship imposes great responsibilities, for which only a full-hearted commitment will suffice. Battles lie ahead, in which few of the decisive encounters will take place on church grounds. The work is urgent; the dangers are real; yet our hearts should be filled with hope. 'Almost thou persuadest me to be a Christian!' Across the gap, that ancient exclamation can still be prompted (in the unlikeliest quarter) by a selfless and compassionate Christian presence. However, a witness of such challenging authority only becomes possible when other transactions, of an intensely personal nature, have taken place earlier . . . Jesus looks at us as He looked at Simon Peter, long ago, and asks the same simple question: '*Lovest thou me?*'